HOW TO BE UP ON DOWN DAYS

HOW TO BE UP ON DOWN *Days*

NELL W. MOHNEY

DIMENSIONS FOR LIVING
NASHVILLE

HOW TO BE UP ON DOWN DAYS

This book is printed on acid-free, recycled paper.

Library of Congress Cataloging-in-Publication Data

Mohney, Nell.
How to be up on down days / Nell W. Mohney.
p. cm.
ISBN 0-687-01781-5 (pbk. : alk. paper)
1. Depressed persons—Religious life. 2. Emotions—Religious aspects—Christianity. 3. Christian life. I. Title.
BV4910.34.M64 1997
248.4—dc21 96-47759
CIP

99 00 01 02 03 04 05 06 — 10 9 8 7 6 5 4

MANUFACTURED IN THE UNITED STATES OF AMERICA

To the men in my life:

my husband, Ralph,

whose optimism and faith in me have pulled me up

on many down days;

and our son,

Ralph Mohney, Jr.,

whose quality of life—including integrity and a great sense of

humor—continues to enable my spirit to soar

CONTENTS

ACKNOWLEDGMENTS

My heartfelt appreciation is expressed to staff members in the reference department of the Chattanooga–Hamilton County Bicentennial Library who have offered assistance both day and night; participants in my seminars throughout the country who have requested such a book; and finally, to all the people whose life experiences are included in this book.

INTRODUCTION

Have you ever had the Monday morning blahs seven days a week? Have you ever felt pulled in all directions? Have you ever felt fragmented, frustrated, overwhelmed? Have you ever wished you could have your spiritual batteries recharged?

If you answered "yes" to any of the above questions, you have had some down days. All of us have had them. It's almost impossible to live in a world of dizzying change and stress without feeling uprooted and powerless at times. The good news is that we don't have to bog down in these feelings. The Christian faith provides us a way to be up on down days.

Some time ago I awakened to one of those days when I simply didn't want to get out of bed. The room was cold, and the electric blanket on my bed was as comforting as a security blanket. I put one foot on the floor, and the other foot said loudly and firmly, "I'm not getting out!"

There was no doubt about it: That was the beginning of a down day. I was physically tired and emotionally discouraged by a difficult relationship that I wasn't sure how to handle. I wanted to stay in bed and pull the covers over my head. Yet I knew that in a little over two hours I was to be the presenter of a seminar in a downtown hotel for a group of business and professional people. Ironically, the subject of the seminar was "How to Motivate Yourself and Others." Just the thought of responsibilities catapulted me out of bed and into my regular early-morning routine, which begins with twenty minutes of vigorous exercise, followed by a quick bath, a quiet time of reading devotional literature, silence, and prayer. Finally, my regimen ends with a high-fiber, low-fat breakfast. If I skip any one of these, I am not adequately prepared to meet the day.

That morning as I dressed, I remembered conversations I had had with seminar participants through the years. In effect, they had said that they seemed to have enough physical, mental, and spiritual resources for the major crises they faced. It was the little things of everyday living—interruptions, irritations, fatigue, lack of motivation, dealing with difficult people—that defeated them. In actuality they were asking, "How can we be up on down days?"

Immediately I thought of two quotations. One was from my spiritual mentor, the late Dr. E. Stanley Jones. Dr. Jones, a missionary to India and an evangelist to America, spoke profound truths succinctly and powerfully. During a speech on the subject of living fully in God's "now," he said: "Life by the yard is hard. Life by the inch is a cinch." The second quotation comes from the Song of Solomon and speaks of "the little foxes that spoil the vines, for our vines have tender grapes" (2:15*b* NKJV). It occurred to me that it is the little things that spoil our days. They dim our vision, dampen our enthusiasm, and cause us to forget the dream of what God wants us to be.

Formula for Being Up on Down Days

On that hard-to-get-out-of-bed day, I began to work out a formula for being up on down days. It is that formula—stop, look, listen, act—that I share with you in this book. This formula provides far more than a superficial approach to life. It has helped me to move out of deep discouragement, to find more joy in life, to overcome anxiety, and to move toward personal freedom. In other words, this formula has helped me to become more spiritually mature.

Consider the words of Jesus, "Be ye therefore perfect, even as your Father which is in heaven is perfect" (Matthew 5:48). The Greek word for *perfect* can be also translated *complete* or *mature.* God wants us to grow up spiritually!

Michelangelo was once asked, "When is a painting finished?" His reply was that it is finished when it fulfills the intent of the artist. By the same measure, a life is complete when it fulfills the purposes of the Creator. Christ points the way to this. He opens our eyes and ears to all that is eternally significant. He puts a sparkle in the eye, a song in the heart, and a bounce in the step. He not only points the way to completeness; he is the Life, as he reminds us in John 14:6: "I am the way, the truth, and the life."

It is important to pause and note that the formula I present in this book is intended for persons who sometimes feel "down"—lethargic, moody, discouraged—not for persons who are seriously depressed. Feeling "down" may come from lack of rest, improper diet, lack of exercise, stress, missed opportunities, hurt feelings, and so forth. Unless we respond to these feelings with positive and faith-filled action, we will, by habit, become unhappy and negative.

Although the formula I suggest will not *hurt* the seriously depressed person, it will not deal with his or her core problem, which may be caused by such things as a chemical imbalance, a traumatic experience, prolonged grief, an addiction, or repressed memories. For those with serious depression, the formula should always be used in conjunction with professional counseling and/or medical advice.

I think of a young woman named Karen, for example, who was discovering a growing inability to function well. She began to lose interest in everything from food and sex to her children's activities and outside social contacts.

Constantly feeling fatigued, she wanted to stay in bed more and more, though she had difficulty getting to sleep and, even then, slept fitfully.

Fortunately, Karen's husband recognized the symptoms of serious depression and found professional help for her. In her case, there was a hormonal imbalance, which could be corrected quickly, plus the repressed memories of physical and verbal abuse, which took a much longer time to erase. Throughout the months of therapy, however, Karen's Christian faith provided inspiration and the powerful belief that she would be made whole. In fact, she has used the terrible experience of what she called "a journey into nowhere" to help others who are experiencing depression. She said, "Throughout the experience I knew that I was not alone, that God was with me. My favorite affirmation became Romans 8:31, 'If God be for [me], who can be against [me]?' "

Getting Started

As the poet William Wordsworth wrote: "The world is too much with us; late and soon, getting and spending, we lay waste our powers." In the frantic pace of today's living, we need to stop often and remember who we are and whose we are. This is not only the beginning point of the formula; it is the key to its success. In order to be anchored and avoid being pushed over by every wind that blows, we need to live with "one foot in heaven."

For me, one of the best ways to do this is to see each day as a gift from God. When I open my eyes in the morning, I try to remember that something brand new has just happened. It has never happened before and will never happen again. This day was dropped at my doorstep as a gift from God. What I do with it will be my gift to him.

The key to being up on down days is to start the day with a spiritual warmup, to expect and plan a good day, to enjoy the day, to make God a vital part of the day, and to end the day with thanksgiving. Throughout the day, I like to use my favorite Bible verse, Psalm 118:24, as an affirmation: "This is the day which the LORD hath made; [I] will rejoice and be glad in it." A poem written by the late Ralph Spaulding Cushman has helped me understand the importance of meeting God early in the morning and "setting our sails" for the day. The last two lines of that poem say it all:

> You must seek Him in the morning
> If you want Him through the day.

We have only one chance at life. God doesn't mean us to live as unhappy, lethargic, defeated participants but as happy, positive, trusting, and energetic Christians. To do this we must stop, look, listen, and act. Join me as we work out the implications of this formula!

I.

Stop

1.

LEARN THE ART OF CENTERING DOWN

As the retreat leader rose to speak, he was bathed in sunlight streaming in from the large windows at the front of the room. The warmth of spiritual sunlight had permeated my soul from time to time throughout the three-day retreat. Yet, here I was on the last morning of the retreat, away from all my usual responsibilities and still churning on the inside. It wasn't anxiety as much as preoccupation. I was thinking about what I had left undone at home and all the things I needed and wanted to do when I returned.

Suddenly a person approached the speaker and handed him a note that said someone had left a car in the parking lot with the motor still running. As the owner of the vehicle left the room, the speaker looked directly at us, smiled, and said, "I wonder how many of you still have your motors running." I knew he was talking directly to me. Perhaps most of the people in the room felt the same way.

The speaker deviated from his planned message to teach us the art of centering down. This is an art perfected by members of the Society of Friends, or Quakers as they are often called. It is a technique that can be used in part, in total, or in varying formats whenever you feel the need to relax. I am suggesting it here as an important part of a quiet time for prayer and meditation, in which you stop and remember who and whose you are.

Breathe Deeply

Deep breathing not only expands our lungs but also sends oxygen to the brain, which helps us to think more clearly. Deep breathing is the first step toward relaxation of your entire body. First, inhale and hold your breath. Feel the tension begin to leave your knotted, stress-filled muscles. When I inhale, I envision the power, peace, and joy of the Lord filling and energizing my body. When I exhale, I envision fear, worry, resentment, and other negative emotions being released from my body and spirit. As I breathe deeply, I say Romans 15:13 in my mind: "Now the God of hope fill you with all joy and peace in believing."

Relax Your Body

Beginning with your feet, flex and relax the muscles in your entire body. As you move up your body, pay special attention to your neck and shoulders, where muscles seem to knot up with stress. Roll your shoulders forward and then backward as if you are rowing a boat. Now bend your head toward your left shoulder. With the fingers of your left hand, stroke the right side of your neck, from your ear down to your collarbone, five times. Do the same on the other side. This is not only wonderful relaxation, but it also opens the lymphatic drainage system.

Don't forget to flex and relax the facial muscles. Then lock your thumbs under your chin and put your index finger above the chin. With short circular motions, move from the center of the chin to the ear. There at the jaw hinge, take your three middle fingers and massage slowly. This helps relieve facial tension and helps to eliminate a double chin.

When you become proficient at this, you can relax your

entire body in one to two minutes. This relaxation procedure not only rids your body of tension but also helps to still your mind. In a boating magazine, I once read: "Ships don't come in on troubled waters." The article described the difficulty of docking a ship during strong winds or troubled waters. It occurred to me that God's creative, empowering thoughts can't come into a fragmented, preoccupied mind. Relaxing our bodies helps to still our minds. "Thou wilt keep him in perfect peace, whose mind is stayed on thee" (Isaiah 26:3).

Practice Stillness and Focus on the Power of God to Bring Tranquillity and Peace

We have a hard time with stillness. For some reason we consider it a greater virtue to be active rather than passive. This is especially true if we are wrestling with a problem. We feel that we ought to be doing something about it instead of first being still to think and to ask God's direction.

Air Force Captain Scott O'Grady was rescued after having been shot down in Bosnia. When he arrived at the Aviano Air Base in Italy, he told how, after parachuting to the ground, his first impulse had been to run. Instead, he became very still, assessed the situation, remembered his training, and prayed. He survived for six days before being rescued by drinking rainwater, eating bugs, and staying quiet so that the enemy forces surrounding him could not detect his position. He said that during that time he also trusted God and the ability of the American armed forces to come to his rescue. Scott O'Grady had developed the ability to focus. We, too, need the ability to focus on the power of God to quiet and renew our minds.

In a fast-moving world, it is easy to be fragmented. We try to sit quietly and remain focused, but our minds move in a million directions. Our inability to focus seems evident even in church. Though we may be engrossed in the music or in the sermon, our eyes automatically seem to follow the late arrival who walks to the front pew. Add a feeling of being down, and it becomes more difficult to focus our minds on God. For me, the answer has always been the Word of God. I affirm those verses that quiet my spirit:

> In quietness and in confidence shall be your strength. (Isaiah 30:15)
>
> Be still, and know that I am God. (Psalm 46:10)
>
> They that wait upon the LORD shall renew their strength; they shall mount up with wings as eagles; they shall run, and not be weary; and they shall walk, and not faint. (Isaiah 40:31)
>
> These things I have spoken unto you, that in me ye might have peace. (John 16:33)

The words of a hymn by John Greenleaf Whittier also help me to center down:

> Drop thy still dews of quietness,
> Till all our strivings cease.
> Take from our souls the strain and stress,
> And let our ordered lives confess the beauty of thy peace.

Remember That the Peace of Christ Brings Harmony Within

Jesus said, "My peace I give unto you" (John 14:27). His peace is the harmony within that keeps us calm and confident in every situation. At this point of centering, I remember someone who counted on this peace. One such person was Horatio Spafford, a Chicago businessman, who was stunned when he learned from the newspaper that the ship carrying his family to Europe in 1873 had sunk in the Atlantic. Two weeks later a cablegram from his wife, Anna, read: "Saved. Alone."

The ship had collided with another vessel near Newfoundland, sinking in twelve minutes. A falling mast stunned Anna, and when she regained consciousness, she learned that all four of their children had gone down with four hundred seventy-four other passengers. She was one of twenty-two passengers who survived, reaching Cardiff, Wales, after two long weeks on the crowded sailing vessel that plucked them from the icy ocean.

Horatio sailed immediately to Wales to be with his wife. When his ship reached the spot where his children had drowned, he wrote these words, which later became a hymn to inspire millions:

> When peace, like a river, attendeth my way,
> When sorrows like sea billows roll;
> Whatever my lot, thou hast taught me to say,
> It is well, it is well with my soul.

Horatio and Anna Spafford made God's peace a part of their lives and later founded and operated the American colony and the Spafford Memorial Children's Hospital in Jerusalem. If they could find peace in their tragedy, then we can find peace amid the pressures, problems, and interruptions of everyday living.

Imagine a Peaceful Place

Finally, I see in my mind's eye a peaceful scene until its quietness envelops me. I like to imagine myself at Camp Carlyle in Hendersonville, North Carolina. It was a camp I attended during my teen years, and it holds happy memories of fun times and spiritual growth. When I am centering down, I see myself seated alone on Vesper Hill, looking down upon a very placid lake.

Soon, my mind is quiet enough to be open to God's creative thoughts. As energy begins to flow again, I can feel myself moving from fragmentation to focused, orderly planning. I feel confident and ready to meet the day. The words of Jesus well up within my heart: "My peace I give unto you: not as the world giveth, give I unto you. Let not your heart be troubled, neither let it be afraid" (John 14:27).

I have a friend who envisions a symphony hall filled with beautiful music as a peaceful scene. Another envisions sitting in the den on a cold winter evening, with a big fire burning in the fireplace. Her husband is sitting in an easy chair, reading. Her children are quietly doing homework. Choose your own peaceful scene.

We live in a fragmented, highly pressured world. One of the survival skills we Christians most need is learning how to relax our bodies and minds. We can do this through the art of centering down. It changes the focus from chaos to the deep and abiding peace of God, "which passes all understanding" (Philippians 4:7 RSV).

Steps for Centering Down

1. Breathe deeply. Inhale God's power, peace, and joy. Exhale fear, worry, resentment, and other negative emotions.

2. Relax your body in order to be rid of physical tension and mental confusion.

3. Practice stillness and focus on the power of God to bring tranquillity and peace. Use scriptural affirmations.

4. Remember that the peace of Christ brings harmony within. Bring to mind a person who has remained peaceful during a difficult situation.

5. Imagine yourself in a peaceful place. Hear Christ saying to you: "My peace I give unto you" (John 14:27). You will be centered, reenergized, and ready to meet the day.

2.

REACH UP AND LIFT OFF

It is the work of Jesus in the world to lift people up who are down. But it can never happen unless we reach up to take his hand. Remember that there are many ways to be down—when we are ill, when we are disappointed, when we are sad, when we are lonely, when we feel guilty, when we are troubled, when we are worried. When we are down in any sense, there is the opportunity to be lifted up by the power and grace of God.

In the Gospel of Mark, there is a story of a woman who was down (see Mark 1:29-31). Simon Peter's mother-in-law was ill. The Greek word that Mark uses to describe her illness means that she had a high fever. After Jesus' long and arduous day of teaching and healing, the disciples told him of her illness, and we read that he "took her by the hand, and lifted her up; and immediately the fever left her" (v. 31).

"Act as If"

Reaching up isn't easy. When we are down, we usually don't feel like doing anything. I can imagine that Peter's mother-in-law didn't feel like putting out her hand to be lifted up. Feelings can bring joy and happiness to our lives, but when they dictate our behavior, they become terrible taskmasters and slave drivers.

The late William James, Harvard professor of sociology and psychology, taught a simple method to keep one from being sabotaged by feelings. It is called "act as if." He said that most of us awaken in the morning and let our feelings determine our actions. If we feel ornery, that's how we act all day; if we feel happy, then we are energized and cheery throughout the day. According to Dr. James, our feelings, not our will or our values, often determine our actions.

His suggestion: Determine our actions on the basis of our values; act that way, and the feelings will follow. I thought of a friend who won a Purple Heart during the Korean War. When I asked if he was frightened during the battle, he replied: "Of course, but I acted courageously and the feelings of courage emerged from someplace."

That must be what Shakespeare meant when he wrote in *Hamlet*, "Assume a virtue, if you have it not"; and what John Wesley, father of the Methodist movement, meant when he said to his young preachers, "Preach faith until you have it, and then preach it because you have it."

Work Through Your Feelings

The "act as if" method doesn't mean that we should disallow feelings. Repressed feelings pop up in strange, unexpected, and often destructive ways. We should be in touch with our feelings if we are to work through them, so that they do not dictate our actions. There are several ways we can do this.

Talking with a Trusted Friend

As Christians, we can process our feelings by talking them out with a trusted friend. As we do this, we begin to see them in perspective. If the friend is wise, he or she will listen attentively and ask questions from time to time. A friend will not give advice unless asked, and then only sparingly. In his book *The Miracle of Dialogue*, Ruel Howe says that we clear away mental confusion and feel empowered when a trusted friend really hears and responds to our feelings.

There also are times when we need to talk with a Christian counselor. If our problem persists, if we suspect we may be overreacting, or if we are unable to think clearly, we need to contact a counselor. Such a person is trained to help us work through our feelings and see options for moving beyond them.

Journaling

A second way to process feelings is through journaling. Sometimes we unconsciously deny our feelings. We rationalize; we justify our reactions; we don't see the situation clearly because we have covered up our true feelings. When I was in high school, I went through a period of criticizing my older sister. I was extremely critical of her clothes, her friends, the apartment into which she and her new husband had moved, and her seeming lack of concern for the family. It was only after writing down my reactions that I saw my real but unconsciously hidden feelings. I was jealous! I envied her freedom—to leave a difficult home situation, to have completed her education and married, to follow a career in teaching, which she loved. At that time, all those opportunities seemed light-years ahead for me, and I was envious that she had already achieved them. Written in black and white, the painful truth became as evident as the nose on my face. The problem belonged to me, not to my sister. This realization could have been devastating to me, except that Christ was also very real in my life. For me, he was not only the historical Jesus but Savior and Friend as well.

Later, I would discover him in two other dimensions: as Lord and as Holy Spirit.

Yet at that difficult time, it was Jesus the Friend and Confidant who helped me through some repressed feelings that could have destroyed my relationship with my sister. Instead, we became great friends. Even today, though she is ill and lives in another city, I see her about once a week.

Prayer

The most important way we work through our feelings is through prayer. In sincere prayer, we receive guidance about what we can do about a problem. After that, we can leave the problem with God, take the hand of Christ, and be lifted up to move on with our lives through his strength. Jesus tells us: "Come to me, all you who are weary and burdened, and I will give you rest" (Matthew 11:28 NIV). Surely Paul had discovered this when he wrote: "I can do all things through Christ who strengthens me" (Philippians 4:13 NKJV).

Remember that prayer is a conversation between two people who love each other. I have found it helpful to begin with gratitude and praise, move to confession, then to requests and intercession for others, and finally to listening. Some of the nudges, such as the need to contact someone, as well as all my creative ideas, seem to come during this valued "listening time." I write down my prayers in a journaling calendar and later make notations when each prayer has been answered—whether or not it was the answer I wanted or anticipated. I encourage you to try it. This simple act will strengthen your faith and surprise you with what the Lord has done in your life.

Ask Yourself If You Need a Spiritual Breakthrough

Years after the difficult period when I resented my sister, Christ again lifted me up and set me upon a new path.

Ironically, I was at one of the lowest points emotionally at a time that should have been one of the happiest in my life. It came during the months following the birth of our first child. Rick had colic for six months and cried almost constantly day and night. We were hundreds of miles away from either set of parents and had little money for baby-sitters. It was my minister husband's first church, and he had only a part-time secretary. Everything else was up to him. As a result, he worked long days and had many meetings at night.

In retrospect, I realize that I was dealing with depression. I was unhappy, unmotivated, irritable, nervous, and resentful of the fresh air my husband breathed. I resented the fact that he could have adult conversations while I was stuck in the house with a crying baby.

Actually, my husband was a wonderful help with the baby. He took all the night shifts with the baby and planned evenings out for us as often as we could afford it. Yet, despite his help and my efforts, I was sinking deeper into depression. I was becoming the kind of person I thoroughly disliked. Eventually I realized that I could not change without divine intervention. Going into the bedroom and closing the door, I knelt beside the bed and poured out my heart to God. The prayer I prayed was wrung from the deepest places of my inner being: "Lord, if you can do anything with this warped personality of mine, you can have it for as long as I live."

When I got up, I didn't feel different (faith is not dependent upon feelings), and the baby was still crying. Even so, I knew something was happening inside me. I was being enveloped in God's love. I decided not to tell anyone about my new commitment, but two days later my husband said, "Did you realize that you are singing for the first time in months?" That day I wrote in my journal: "When we touch even the hem of his garment in desperate, believing faith, we too will be made whole again." Though I haven't always walked in daily fellowship with Christ, I have always known when I was out of fellowship with him. In these times I have missed the inner peace so urgently that I have quickly sought to return.

There is a vast difference between feeling "down" or discouraged and being depressed. Some of the symptoms of depression include loss of interest in normal activities, lack of concern for personal appearance, loss of appetite, obsessive eating, change in sleep patterns—sleeping too much or insomnia—and a feeling of hopelessness.

Any two or more of these symptoms should send you immediately to the doctor for a physical checkup. If symptoms persist after you have followed your doctor's advice, make an appointment with a Christian counselor. My own spiritual breakthrough came only after a thorough physical exam and a number of sessions with a competent and caring Christian counselor.

Reach Up or Bog Down

When we refuse to take Christ's offered hand and, instead, become the victim of our feelings and moods, we bog down in self-centeredness, resulting in bitterness, unhappiness, and anger. Once on a flight from the Midwest, I sat beside a woman whose husband had died of a sudden heart attack years ago. I quickly learned that ever since her husband's death she had felt nothing but despair and had put her life and happiness on hold. From her comments, I gathered that she talked about the experience constantly and showed no interest in people around her—even her children and grandchildren. It seemed to me that she had not reached up for the hand of Christ or desired to be lifted up. Her world had become a self-centered cocoon of despair from which she couldn't seem to emerge. She had not allowed the light of Christ to enter her world of darkness. Hence, she could do nothing to bring light to others.

Just the opposite was true of my mother-in-law, Mrs. S. P. Mohney, of Lexington, Kentucky. She was a woman of gentility and refinement. She loved music, poetry, and beauty in every form. Her rose gardens were a place of quiet beauty. Flower arrangements graced her home and were the centerpiece for holiday meals, which were as attractively served as they were delicious. The center of her life was her church, her physician husband, and her four sons.

Being part of a generation of women who never worked outside the home and whose husbands handled all the financial affairs, my mother-in-law was very dependent. We wondered how she would manage after her husband's death. Later we discovered there was no need for our concern. She faced the future and planned for it. After she took time for mourning, she decided it was time to move from the big house into an apartment; and she chose the apartment herself. Though her husband had handled the finances, she made it her business to learn what the situation was, so there was no financial chaos or indecision. In addition, she stayed involved in her sons' families, traveling to see us for short trips and inviting us to her home for holidays. She also stayed involved in church activities, in garden clubs, and with her friends. She told me one day that her husband's death was the most terrible loss of her life, but that strength had come to her through her faith in Christ. She remembered his words: "I will never leave you nor forsake you" (Hebrews 13:5 NKJV). Through her Christian faith she had the sure knowledge that she would see "Doc" again.

My observation is that even the most committed Christians sometimes struggle with discouragement and depression. In fact, most of us would have to admit that we are guilty of this occasionally. I seem most vulnerable when I am feeling very tired or stressed, or when I am discouraged. There is a legend that Satan once said to his assistants: "Be sure that you never lose or give away one special tool. That tool is discouragement, because it is the one that most easily defeats the Christian."

So what are we to do? My suggestion is that we practice an especially good health regimen during these times: Exercise daily, get plenty of rest, eat nutritious food, interrupt negative thought patterns (under stress, we often revert to old, negative patterns of fear and worry), and remember that we are not alone. Unfortunately, there are some people who, because of their physical or emotional makeup, will always be subject to bouts of depression. These people especially need to remember that God's grace will sustain them as they go through their valleys.

Concentrate on Your Assets

Another thing that has helped me when I am down or depressed is to count my blessings or, in other words, to concentrate on my assets. It is so easy to focus on our problems or on what we have lost. Instead, our focus needs to be on what we have left.

We lost our oldest son when he was twenty. He had a motorcycle accident and died ten days later. I had a terrible time with my grief. I learned how quickly all my thoughts were focused on Rick's death, on what I had lost. My grief did not begin to lift until I read and practiced the words of Paul in 1 Thessalonians 5:18: "In every thing give thanks." He was saying that even in the midst of pain and grief, I needed to move my focus from what I had lost to what I had left. I needed to concentrate on my assets.

From then on, I began each day by conditioning my mind with gratitude. I thanked God for a husband who loved me; for another son who was alive and well; for friends; for faith; for a job that demanded my best thought. Little by little my grief began to lift. In fact, that process so revolutionized my life that I continue it to this day. On the rare occasions when I oversleep and don't condition my mind with gratitude, I find myself irritable with others and impatient with myself.

This is a good practice even when things are going great, because it conditions our minds and "sets our sails" for the day. Some years ago I read a book titled *The First Four Minutes.* The premise of the book is that the first four minutes in almost every situation make a tremendous difference in the outcome. The author said, for example, that when we meet a new person, we decide in the first four minutes whether we want to pursue the relationship. When a husband and wife see each other after a day's work, the first four minutes they are together will set the climate for the evening. Certainly, if we focus on our blessings when we awaken, we are creating the climate for a positive, happy day.

Take an Aspirin and Read the Twenty-Third Psalm

When London was under almost constant bombing attack during World War II, the people were frustrated, overstressed, and frightened. Often they went for days without sleep; their nerves were on edge. Doctors' offices were jammed. A member of the English parish that my husband served during a ministerial exchange some years ago told us that his doctor often gave this prescription during the war: "Take two aspirin, drink a glass of warm milk, read the Twenty-third Psalm, and go to bed."

In essence, the British doctor was saying that we should use help from the medical community when we are ill or depressed. The aspirin was symbolic of that. Then we should use common sense and take care of our bodies. Drinking warm milk and going to bed were symbolic of that. Finally, we should allow the peace and power of faith to restore our souls. The Twenty-third Psalm was symbolic of that. In other words, we must reach up and lift off.

When we are young, we usually carry a blueprint in our minds of what our lives will be. We don't go very far, however, until we find roadblocks, detours, illnesses, even tragedies in our paths. All of us will have reason to feel down or experience depression. At these times let us remember that Jesus said, "In the world you will have tribulation; but be of good cheer, I have overcome the world" (John 16:33 NKJV). Here's a simple formula to remember when we hit the roadblocks: Think calmly, follow a sensible health regimen, get medical help if needed, and "Trust in the LORD with all your heart, and lean not on your own understanding; in all your ways acknowledge Him, and He shall direct your paths" (Proverbs 3:5-6 NKJV).

Steps for Centering Down

1. Remember that it is the work of Jesus to lift people up who are down.

2. Affirm that being down gives you the opportunity to be lifted up by the power and grace of God.

3. Remember that when you are down, it is your job to reach up and take the offered hand of Christ.

4. Recognize that reaching up isn't easy, and then "act as if."

5. Work through and process your feelings by talking with a trusted friend or counselor, journaling, and praying.

6. Concentrate on your assets and give thanks.

7. Take care of your physical needs and read the Twenty-third Psalm.

3.

LIGHTEN UP WITH LAUGHTER

She looked like an army drill sergeant—with a sturdy build, abrupt speech, and a take-charge, no-nonsense manner. This airport restaurant waitress charged through the kitchen door and approached her customer with an "I need your order now" attitude.

One of her customers was a mild-mannered, distinguished-looking, gray-haired pastor who had been the featured speaker at a large gathering in the city the day before. He was taking an early-morning flight back to his home. On that particular morning, he may have been sleepy or preoccupied with thoughts of his day's activities. At any rate, the burly waitress evidently perceived him as tense, even dour, because as she descended on his table she said in a loud, gruff voice, "Lighten up, buttercup!"

When the pastor told that story at a recent gathering, the participants were convulsed with laughter. In the first place, the thought of such a distinguished gentleman being called "buttercup" was so ridiculous that it was funny. Even more humorous was the fact that he told it on himself, and with such vivid description that we could see that substantial woman and almost smell the coffee she poured as she made that impertinent remark.

As I have reflected on the incident, I have come to the conclusion that in a world full of pressures and deadlines, most of us would do well to lighten up and laugh more.

The Bible Encourages Laughter

I have always enjoyed the biblical story of aged Abraham and Sarah doubled up with laughter on being told that they were to have a baby. Even God laughed with them. The miracle child who was born to them was named Isaac, which means laughter.

Often I have wondered if the Creator of the universe does not laugh when we strut around with feelings of imperial self-importance and self-sufficiency. He must, however, be more saddened than amused when we forget our dependence upon him, or when we forget that we, like Abraham and Sarah, can accomplish unbelievable things when we claim his promises and seek to fulfill his purposes. Perhaps many of us should hear him say to us, "Lighten up, buttercup."

Dr. Charles Swindoll writes in his book *Maybe It's Time to Laugh Again,*

> God's sense of humor has intrigued me for years. After all, he made you and me, didn't He? And what about all those funny looking creatures that keep drawing us back to the zoo? . . . God must have smiled when Elijah mocked the false prophets on Mount Carmel, asking whether their gods had gone on a long journey or fallen asleep or were indisposed (1 Kings 18:27). And what about that fellow Eutychus who listened to Paul preach and fell out of a third-story window (Acts 20:9). Don't tell me God didn't find humor in that scenario.

Solomon reminds us that even in laughter the heart may ache (Proverbs 14:13), but humor gives us a needed break from the pain of heartache. When we forget our dependence upon Christ or fail to remember what we can accomplish through his power, we need to "lighten up" and heed Paul's words: "I can do all things through Christ who strengthens me" (Philippians 4:13 NKJV).

In his book *The Humor of Christ,* Elton Trueblood tells us that Jesus said it is impossible to enter the kingdom of God unless we become as little children (Mark 10:15). He points out that a part of childlikeness is playfulness and the ability to laugh. Even Christ had a sense of humor. His humor often involved paradox—"the blind lead the blind" (Luke 6:39)—and exaggeration—"It is easier for a camel to go through the eye of a needle, than for a rich man to enter into the kingdom of God" (Mark 10:25). Obviously, Jesus had a marvelous maturity that included both seriousness and laughter. He didn't use humor to make people laugh but to help them see and remember the truths of the kingdom. Most of all, Jesus emphasized the importance of joy and balanced living: "These things have I spoken unto you, that my joy might remain in you, and that your joy might be full" (John 15:11).

Laughter Is Good Medicine

"A merry heart doeth good like a medicine" (Proverbs 17:22). From Aristotle to Kant to Locke, the power of laughter has been taught through the ages. In recent years, the physical benefits of laughter have received much attention. Norman Cousins, who served as editor of *Saturday Review* for many years, laughed himself back to health and wrote about it in *The Anatomy of an Illness.* He witnessed the curative power of laughter in dealing with his life-threatening illness. Part of his rehabilitation regimen was to rent old Laurel and Hardy movies and watch them for several hours each day. Not only was this a distraction from pain and a spirit lifter, but it actually helped to strengthen his immune system. Later he was invited to join the staff of a medical school, where he helped patients understand the role of positive attitudes and laughter in their recovery.

Many physical benefits of laughter have been studied and documented. Laughter can lower your blood pressure and heart rate, lower your stress level, improve relationships and emotional stability, improve diaphragmatic breathing, improve the flow of blood to the brain, restore your interest and energy, and stimulate creativity. In addition, you will enjoy life more and be more fun to be around.

I know of a woman whose husband was killed suddenly in an automobile crash. They had three children. Both parents were persons of steadfast Christian faith who practiced joy and laughter in their daily lives. Though the family went through a period of grieving after his death, the mother was able to continue some of the fun things they had done as a means of remembering him and coping with their grief. Laughter helped to erase their pain.

Three Simple Steps to Laughter

In his book *Maybe It's Time to Laugh Again,* Dr. Charles Swindoll writes that the three biggest joy killers are worry, stress, and fear. Though we can't control many of the circumstances of our lives, we can, with the help of God, control our reactions. If we are a fearful, stressed-out worrier, we can begin to laugh again by following three simple steps.

1. Look for Humor in Everyday Life

This doesn't mean telling jokes, but creating a state of fun or play. Comedian Steve Martin says that he gets his laughter juices going each morning by looking at himself in the mirror when he first gets out of bed, which, he says, is good for about three or four minutes of hilarity. Of course, it wouldn't be healthy to laugh at our physical appearance every morning, but we can begin each day with laughter and carry a light spirit throughout the day.

Motivational speaker and author Mamie McCullough has a marvelous ability to see humor in everyday events. She endears herself to readers and audiences by her ability to laugh at herself. I once heard her tell of an embarrassing experience. She explained that after she speaks, she usually goes to the restroom, freshens up, and then gets something to eat. When she speaks in her home state of Texas, she travels by car instead of by plane. Her habit is to stop at the nearest McDonalds after speaking.

After many such stops, she has learned that in Texas, the ladies' restroom at McDonalds is always on the right side of the restaurant. The stops have become so habitual that she even stopped looking at the sign on the door. One day she was speaking in an adjacent state and literally ran into a nearby McDonalds. Automatically, she turned into the restroom on the right. To her amazement, four men were in the room. As she told about the incident, she said, "I don't know why I felt I ought to explain, but I did. The only thing I could think of to say was, 'My husband just left me, and I'm looking everywhere for him.' " What comic relief for a bad situation!

My husband and I receive many church bulletins and enjoy reading the "bloopers" from typographical errors or sentence construction. For example: "The choir will meet at the Larson home for fun and sinning"; "This afternoon there will be a meeting in the north and south ends of the church and children will be christened at both ends"; "Smile at someone who is hard to love; say hell to someone who doesn't care much about you"; "For those of you who have children and don't know it, we have a nursery downstairs."

There is humor all around us. All we have to do is look for it!

2. When You Feel Yourself Getting Irritated or Angry, Count to Ten and Then Try to See Something Ludicrous in the Situation

This will either clear your perspective or help you to deal with the situation more calmly. Either way, you will realize that whatever it was, it was not worth getting upset about.

In 1987 at the American Football Conference play-offs, the Denver Broncos were playing the Cleveland Browns in Cleveland. It was near the end of the fourth quarter, and Cleveland had just scored. They were one touchdown ahead. Only one minute and fifty-seven seconds remained in the game. At the next kickoff, Denver fumbled the ball on its own one-yard line, and spectators assumed the game was over. Denver fans groaned and bemoaned the loss; hostile Cleveland fans threw dog biscuits on the field; even the announcers were speculating about who Cleveland would play in the Super Bowl.

Time-out was called, and John Elway and the Broncos went into a huddle in their own end zone. In that tense, seemingly hopeless situation, Keith Bishop, the all-American left tackle, said with a twinkle in his eye: "Hey guys, now we've got 'em just where we want 'em." It was such a ludicrous statement that the whole team burst out laughing. One player laughed so much that he fell on the ground.

In that moment, laughter relieved anxiety and tension and infused the team with calm confidence. What followed has become known in football annals as "the drive." The Broncos regained the ball and drove down the field to score in the last seconds of the game. They won the game in overtime and went to the 1988 Super Bowl.

It has been said that "laughter is our best weapon and the one least used." It is true. How many of us consciously use humor to relieve tension and help us deal with problems?

3. Remember That Some of Our Concerns Are "Much Ado About Nothing"

Their outcomes will make no difference in ten years. Though we must right the wrongs, the weight of the world is not on our shoulders. God is still in control. So we can laugh and love and trust God for the future.

Early one morning I was hard at work in my office at the church. Suddenly the door flew open and in walked a young woman, sobbing uncontrollably. Sally was one of the active young adults of our church. She was attractive, intelligent, had a good job, and had just celebrated her first wedding anniversary.

Judging from her sobs, I thought she and Tim must have a serious relationship problem or that someone close to her had died. Finally, when she was able to stop crying and talk, she said that she and Tim had not been included on the guest list for a big party given by the supervisor in Tim's company.

"This must mean that Tim isn't doing well, because everybody else in his department was invited," she said. "Also, we had this couple to dinner just a month ago, and now they've 'snubbed' us. It's just not fair!"

Though it seemed to me that she had blown the whole thing out of proportion, I knew that Sally was feeling the pain of rejection. So I let her talk through her feelings.

Then I asked, "Are you sure that you and Tim are the only couple in the department who were excluded?" No, she wasn't sure after all. In fact, she knew of only two in the department who were invited. "Then this had nothing to do with Tim's competence or reputation at work," I suggested. She nodded.

"And haven't there been times," I asked, "when you couldn't include everyone you'd like on an invitation list?"

"Of course," she said, "but we had that couple for dinner just last month." Suddenly she grinned and said, "Guess I'm just dealing with hurt pride."

I smiled and reminded her, "Well, the pain of rejection can be very real, and all of us have to face it from time to time." By then she was able to look at things more objectively.

She straightened her shoulders, dried her tears, and headed out for another appointment, calling to me, "Thanks for helping me to see that this was not the end of the world."

As she left, I thought of how often we spend hours worrying and crying over something that won't matter at all ten years from now. Incidentally, Tim later became president of that company!

Learn to Laugh at Yourself

We receive a subtle but wonderful benefit from the ability to laugh at ourselves. It helps us to see ourselves in proper perspective—to realize that no matter what our credentials, we are not the center of the universe.

When I was first married, I couldn't cook. Actually, I told my husband this before we were married. Later he told me he had thought all girls said that so that the husband would be surprised when his new wife presented her first meal. Well, my husband was certainly surprised!

You see, when I was growing up, my mother didn't like people in the kitchen when she was cooking. I had washed a billion dishes and done other household chores, but I had never put a meal together.

Three weeks before I was married, mother was stricken in her conscience. She took me into the kitchen and taught me to make one meal. It was fried chicken, mashed potatoes, green beans, and congealed salad—orange Jell-O with carrots and pineapple.

I do not exaggerate when I tell you that when we returned from our wedding trip, we had the same meal every day for three weeks—except for breakfast. For breakfast we had cold cereal and toast. But for lunch and dinner we had fried chicken, mashed potatoes, green beans, and congealed salad. I didn't even change the color of the Jell-O. Even now when we attend a covered dish dinner, my husband shies away from that orange Jell-O.

Finally one Saturday, he said to me, "Do you think we could have baked chicken tomorrow?"

Quickly I replied, "Of course. You go buy the chicken and I will bake it." While he was at the grocery store, I telephoned my neighbor and asked, "Geneva, how do you bake a chicken?"

She told me some things that I don't do now. She said: "Get out your roaster; put in water, the chicken, salt and pepper, and then put the lid on. While the oven is heating, turn on the eyes on the top of the stove and set the roaster there." The next morning after breakfast, I did everything she had suggested, and then I went into the bedroom to dress for church. My husband was in the study putting the finishing touches on his sermon. The only thing I had failed to tell my neighbor was that my roaster was glass, not Pyrex.

In about five minutes there was a terrible explosion in the kitchen. It sounded like fireworks going off at Disney World. We both rushed to the kitchen door, and that scene is indelibly imprinted in my mind. The stove was steaming, water was running all over the kitchen floor, glass was in every corner of the room, and the uncooked chicken was under the table.

I said to myself, *I am sure he must be thinking he married the dumbest girl in the world. What's he going to do?* What he did was burst out laughing. It was not a quiet, gentle laugh, but a sidesplitting one. That sound was wonderful! The whole situation changed.

I exclaimed, "You look better to me right now than the night we were married, but what are we going to do? The

The Benefits of Laughter

1. Laughter helps us to stay physically healthy and to fight disease. Laughter is like internal aerobics. Our circulation and heart rate are improved; our blood pressure is lowered; our immune system is strengthened; we are distracted from pain.

2. Laughter improves our relationships.

3. Laughter restores our energy and interests and stimulates our creativity.

4. Laughter helps us enjoy life more.

5. Laughter relaxes us and lifts our spirits.

6. Laughter makes us more flexible and optimistic.

7. Laughter gives us a needed break from the pain of heartache.

8. Laughter helps us to deal constructively with problems and difficult situations.

stove won't work; we don't have any money; we don't even have peanut butter."

As he put his arm around me, he said, "There is just one thing to do: Go to church and look hungry." Actually, it must have worked. While I was shaking hands with a member after church, she said, "We have wanted to take you and your husband out to eat since you were married. Could you possibly go to lunch with us today?"

As I smiled, I replied demurely, "I'll see if my husband has anything planned." Inside I was saying, *Thank you, Lord!* That could have been a traumatic experience for a newly married couple. Instead, my husband's laughter drew us closer and turned the incident into a great conversation starter.

A word of warning so that the ability to laugh at ourselves gives balance and perspective to our lives: Laughing at ourselves should never mean belittling, demeaning, or putting ourselves down. The latter can decimate a good self-image.

Laughter Makes You a Better Person

It is my observation that the people who laugh easily are those who are more understanding, more relaxed, more optimistic, and much more flexible. Several years ago I went to hear a well-known speaker. I had worked hard to clear my schedule and save enough time for the drive to the city where she was speaking. When I returned home, my husband asked eagerly, "Well, how did you like her? Did you enjoy the speech?"

Sadly, I had to admit that I agreed with everything she said, but the whole experience was a downer. It was too intense! She never smiled or laughed or told a humorous incident. As a result, I was exhausted at the end of the hour. Granted, I, and perhaps most of the women present, needed to confront some of the truths presented that day, but as the saying goes, "A little bit of sugar helps the medicine go down." A little bit of laughter that day would have made the truth much easier to accept.

Those who laugh easily, who don't take themselves too seriously, and who look for the humor in life are not only healthier, happier people; they are more fun to be around! Laughter can actually bring you more friends, which, in turn, brings you more opportunities for experiencing joy. When you consider the many benefits of laughter, it may be one of the simplest and most effective ways to be up on down days!

Steps for Lightening Up with Laughter

1. As you read the Bible, keep a running list of the references to laughter and joy. You will agree with Nehemiah, "The joy of the LORD is your strength" (Nehemiah 8:10).

2. When you are tempted to be gloomy and discouraged, remember Proverbs 17:22: "A merry heart doeth good like a medicine: but a broken spirit drieth the bones."

3. If you are a fearful, stressed-out worrier, you can begin to laugh again by three simple steps: (1) Look for humor in everyday life; (2) When you feel yourself getting irritated or angry, count to ten and then try to see something ludicrous in the situation; (3) Ask yourself if the outcome of your concern will make any difference ten years from now.

4. Learn to laugh at yourself. No matter how impressive your credentials, you are not the center of the universe.

5. Remember that laughter should never demean yourself or be used as sarcasm or ridicule of another.

6. Remember that when you laugh easily, you will be more relaxed, more flexible, more optimistic, more approachable, and hence more fun to be around.

4.

PRIORITIZE AND ORGANIZE

The doorbell rang. *Oh no*, I thought, *not another interruption in an already hectic day*. Rick, age four, had just spilled finger paint on the kitchen floor, and Ralph, age two, was screaming from the playpen. I answered the door out of breath to let the person on the other side know that I was already out of time. At the door stood my neighbor, Mary Ann, looking calm, cool, and collected. My impulse was to slam the door and run inside and hide. After all, Mary Ann was only two years older than I, but she was light-years ahead of me in ordered living. As a frazzled and often frustrated young mother, I looked with admiration as her three squeaky-clean children ran boisterously but happily into the yard to play. Whether she was dealing with unexpected company or children falling out of the oak tree, she seemed unflappable. All those thoughts ran through my mind as I invited her to come in. Thankfully, she declined, saying, "Sorry. I don't have time just now, but I baked chocolate-chip cookies this morning and thought you and the boys might enjoy them." Then she was off again, and I stood holding a plate of warm cookies and wondering how Mary Ann managed to accomplish so much. I also wondered if she ever had a down day.

Several weeks later we had a long talk, and I was able to pose that question to my friend. In addition to being Christian and centered in Christ at the core of her being, Mary Ann gave me three practical suggestions for coping with down days: Don't take on more than you can do; don't procrastinate; and organize your week on Sunday afternoon.

I discovered that she was right. A down day can result if we take on more than we can do, if we tend to procrastinate, or if we lack organization and are not prepared for what needs to be done. When we are unprepared, overcommitted, or disorganized, we are likely to feel overwhelmed. That in itself makes us want to run away or pull the covers over our heads.

The Gift of Time

Recently I was waiting at a traffic light to cross the street when a young man asked, "What time have you?" I told him what time it was, but his phrasing of the question lingered in my mind and reminded me of my conversation with Mary Ann so many years ago. It also enlarged my appreciation for the gift of time.

What time have you? Of course, no one knows whether we have a day, a month, a year, or the biblical "threescore and ten" on the planet Earth. What we do know is that like the children of Israel in the wilderness receiving daily manna, God gives us only one day's supply of time. There is absolute justice in the gift of time: No person receives more than another, though I was sure that Mary Ann got an extra supply occasionally.

Neither can we save nor hoard time as we do money. For example, we can't save an extra hour from today or two from next week and put them in a "time bank" so that we can cash in on a particularly crowded day. There is no way we can save five years—or add five minutes—to our life expectancy. Every bit of our time allotted for today will have to be used by midnight tonight.

Matthew's Gospel records Jesus' thoughts on the importance of living one day at a time: "Take therefore no thought for the morrow: for the morrow shall take thought for the things of itself. Sufficient unto the day is the evil thereof" (6:34). The late Dr. William Ousler, once head of the Johns Hopkins School of Medicine, was speaking to students at Yale University and suggested that they learn to live in day-tight compartments. He reported that many lives are sabotaged by trying to deal with the regrets of yesterday and the anxieties of tomorrow while living in today.

His suggestion is affirmed by the ancient words of wisdom from the Sanskrit:

> Look to this day
> For it is life, the very life of life.
> In its brief course lie all the
> Verities and realities of your existence:
>   the bliss of growth
>   the glory of action
>   the splendor of beauty
> Look well, therefore, to this day!

Overcome Procrastination

Because time is so precious, we need to learn to use it wisely. In his letter to the Ephesians, Paul suggested that they "redeem the time" (see 5:16). In order to do this, we must recognize the limits of time. The challenge of a football game is that it doesn't go on for days. Whatever a team is going to do must be done in four quarters. That's it! In baseball there are nine innings—not ninety nine; in golf you play nine or eighteen holes and then "tally up." We have only one chance at life, and this is it. Fortunately for us, we can make corrections and even change courses as we go along, but we can't buy an extension of time. Knowing that, we should never take life for granted but should remember the words of the psalmist: "So teach us to number our days, that we may apply our hearts unto wisdom" (Psalm 90:12). In other words, we should remember to enjoy and appreciate the current season of our lives and to seek God's guidance daily.

Unfortunately, most of us put things off, thinking we can do them tomorrow. Yet all we really have is today. Someone has said: "Yesterday is history; tomorrow is a mystery; today is a gift. That's why we call it 'the present.' "

The CEO of a large company in my city has a bud vase on his desk in which he keeps a stem with several thorns in it. When I asked about it, he told me it was a reminder not to procrastinate but to deal with problems as they arise. He said, "If you touch the thorn tentatively, it will prick you; but if you grasp it all at once, it doesn't hurt at all." When we fail to do things that need to be done, we soon live with a sense of impending doom, which certainly doesn't allow us to feel "up." In addition, procrastination causes us to feel stressed out, inferior, incompetent, and irritable.

We overcome procrastination by daily planning, organization, and making up our minds to be decisive, even if all our decisions are not good ones. This doesn't mean that our decisions aren't thoughtful. We need to weigh the pros and cons of the decisions we make, but the time comes when, as the fisherman says, "It's time to fish or cut bait."

Procrastination often comes from perfectionism. Some of us want everything to be perfect. But in this world, everything won't be perfect. It is especially important to remember that there are acceptable compromises for balance. There is a difference between seeking excellence and seeking perfection. Excellence is a worthy goal; perfectionism is not. If we insist on controlling everything, then we not only find ourselves fragmented and fatigued, but we also create false guilt in persons around us.

Learn to Say "No"

Susan was tired when she awakened. Last night she had stayed up far too late preparing posters for her civic club. She resented the president for asking her to do so much, and she resented herself for not being assertive enough to say "no."

Before she drove her three children to kindergarten and elementary school and then herself to work, she had to prepare a covered dish for a church dinner that evening. She often wished the church dinners were catered, but as a single parent, she probably wouldn't be able to afford it. That morning one child forgot his books and lunch money, so she had to drive six extra blocks to retrieve them. She was late to work and feeling panicky even before she saw on her desk a report that was not her responsibility but that she had foolishly promised to complete for a coworker. She wanted to scream and tear up things. There was no doubt about it: Her life was out of control.

It can happen to any of us. Pressures mount, responsibilities increase, a worker doesn't show up to make a repair, unexpected company arrives, and we find ourselves out of control. How can we avoid this? One way is to learn to say "no" without feeling guilty. At times, all of us take on more than we can handle, which causes us to feel fragmented and overwhelmed. However, if we consistently do this, we need to take a close look at what is going on in our lives.

If, for example, we have a bad self-image; if we are children of an alcoholic parent; if we are perfectionists; if we have been abused; or if, for any reason, we feel insecure, we may have an inordinate need to please people. Because of this need, we constantly take on more things than we can handle and end up feeling inundated and often resentful of the people who made the requests.

For many years this was a problem for me. A bad self-image plus the demands I placed upon myself as a minister's wife made me feel that I needed to respond to everyone's expectations. The perfectionist in me made me try to do everything well. As a result, I felt pressured and pulled in many directions. I was driven and couldn't enjoy life without feeling guilty.

Learning to say "no" without giving long explanations has been very freeing to me. In those insecure days, I felt I owed everyone an explanation if I couldn't grant a request. That in itself was another evidence of my lack of confidence. After all, people don't want an explanation. They want a "yes" or "no." It is sufficient to say simply and sincerely, "I wish I could help you, but it is just not possible right now." How liberating it was to learn that!

Assert Yourself Confidently

Three things that helped me to overcome my inability to assert myself confidently and say "no" when I needed to can also help you.

1. Draw Support from a Loving Relative or Friend

Fortunately, I had a husband who believed in me, affirmed me, and helped me liberate my gifts and talents. He helped me see that as a mother of small children, I had neither the time nor the energy to work in youth ministries as I had in the past. He suggested that, instead, I accept an invitation to teach a young adult class. It was an eye-opening experience. I came to see that my spiritual gift and natural talent is really teaching through speaking and writing. Because I believe that Christians should use their gifts in ministry for Christ, I was delighted to focus on the one thing that I did best, rather than try to be all things to all people. My reading and study became a time of personal growth and joy. A sense of deep inner peace began to settle over me as I finally "came home to myself."

Of course, this focus didn't prevent me from occasionally helping with dinners at the church or helping a family in need. We all must fulfill our responsibility to live as Christians in love and service to others. Neither did finding my spiritual gift and having an opportunity to use it keep me from feeling fragmented at times. There always will be choices between the good, the better, and the best. What it did for me was give me a sense of direction and focus. More and more I realized what God was calling me to be and do. By recognizing and accepting the gift of teaching that God has given me, I have had the wonderful opportunity to write and speak to business, professional, and church groups all across the country.

As we learn to assert ourselves and say "no" appropriately, a loving relative or friend can provide the security that enables us to face ourselves honestly and make some hard decisions without feeling like a failure. One of the ways they do this is through total acceptance. There is a wonderful freedom that comes when we realize that we are accepted just as we are, not for what we have achieved. Also, it gives us the opportunity to express honest appreciation and encouragement (not flattery). To encourage another means to "put heart into." To discourage means to "take heart out of."

If you are surrounded by negative people at home or at work, it can be easy to allow them to color your thoughts. Don't give in to their negativity. Instead, keep your mind saturated with positive thoughts from inspirational tapes or books. A few you may find helpful are *The Power of Positive Thinking* and *A Guide to Confident Living* by Norman Vincent Peale; *The Power of Optimism* by Alan L. McGinnis; *Tough Times Never Last but Tough People*

Do by Robert Schuller; and my own *Don't Put a Period Where God Put a Comma.* In addition, seek a new friend who is positive and hopeful.

2. Recognize and Affirm Your Identity as a Christian

As my awareness of my identity as a Christian grew, I realized that I didn't need to prove my worth to anyone. I was already a person of worth because of what Christ had done for me. This was powerfully affirmed for me through Scripture verses such as these: "For God so loved the world, that he gave his only begotten Son, that whosoever believeth in him should not perish, but have everlasting life" (John 3:16); "Ye have not chosen me, but I have chosen you, and ordained you, that ye should go and bring forth fruit" (John 15:16).

This realization didn't happen overnight. It came as I intentionally took advantage of spiritual growth and renewal. Even now when I am tired, I experience some of the old familiar feelings of inadequacy. It is then that I affirm my Christian heritage: Created in the image of God, redeemed by Christ, and empowered by the Holy Spirit. This is a powerful image and heritage! To claim it means to internalize the meaning in our thoughts, expectations, and attitudes, and then to live it in the nitty-gritty of life. When we claim our Christian heritage, we have an inner gyroscope that enables us to determine our direction and choose priorities. And when we believe we are persons of worth and want to please God, we don't have the need to please others as much.

3. Learn to Organize Your Time at the Beginning of Each Week

I learned from my neighbor Mary Ann the importance of organizing my week on Sunday afternoon. That simple organizational procedure helps me to plan my week in advance so that I don't duplicate efforts and run around in circles.

How well I remember one week when I didn't do it. It was a rainy afternoon, and because I was unorganized, I ended up driving across town three times to do what could have been accomplished, with a little preplanning, in one trip. Each time I got into the car, I had to interrupt small children at play, dress them in rainwear, and try to soothe their irritation. If I had planned my week on Sunday, I would have known that I didn't have enough meat for dinner on Tuesday and that I needed to pick up cleaning and a birthday gift. I could have felt "up" instead of frazzled, overwhelmed, and irritated.

That experience helped me to recognize the importance of becoming disciplined in organizing my life. In fact, I have observed that being organized plays a large part in freeing us from the stress that can overwhelm us and lead to down days.

Three Things That Can Help You Assert Yourself Confidently

1. A person who believes in you, affirms you, and helps you to liberate your gifts and talents.

2. A growing awareness of your identity as a Christian: "I am a person of worth because of what God has done for me."

3. Learning to organize your time at the beginning of each week.

Know Your Priorities

The first step in organizing your life is knowing what your priorities are. Volumes have been written through the years about how to do this. In the early days of time-management seminars, the emphasis was on making lists and setting short- and long-term goals. Though these certainly have a place in good time management, if taken to extremes they can enslave us to a system. It is possible to become a "time nut," to allow the trivial and urgent to become the important, to become efficient instead of effective.

It was in a business seminar some years ago that business consultant Peter Drucker proposed an idea that has revolutionized my planning. He suggested that before we set short-term and long-term goals, we must determine our ultimate goals, or where we want to be when we "get there."

In his popular book *Seven Habits of Highly Effective People,* Dr. Stephen Covey suggests something similar in his chapter titled "Put First Things First." First he asks you to go in your imagination to a funeral home. After speaking to friends, you go into a room where the casket is open. To your surprise, you see yourself in the casket. This is your funeral three months hence. Speaking at the service will be a family member, a friend, a colleague from work, and a person with whom you have done volunteer work in the community. What would you like them to say? How do you want to be remembered?

These two suggestions caused me to look long and prayerfully at my life and my "soul's sincere desires." After a bit of fine tuning, I came up with four ultimate goals: 1) to be an authentic Christian; 2) to give and receive love, especially to the "significant others" in my life; 3) to use my two talents, speaking and writing, to inspire and help others; 4) to go to heaven when I die. This has simplified my life in wonderful ways. Though I still have to decide between good, better, and best options, the trivial can be eliminated without qualms. Now I know, for example, to focus my training opportunities on speaking and writing skills, rather than on something that will not contribute to my four goals. Most important, it has made me realize that I don't need a master plan for my life, but I do need to be in the Master's Plan.

Dr. Joyce Brothers says that if you are having problems deciding what you want, you should use the quick-list test. Once a week, at the same time (she suggests Saturday morning), ask yourself what you deeply want in life. Write whatever comes to mind without questioning it. Do this for six weeks, go over the list, and write down the things that appear on every list. These, she concludes, are your "soul's sincere desires."

When I do this exercise, I also ask myself two questions: Is there anything on this list that will hurt me or anyone else? Is there anything on the list that is not in keeping with the will of God as exemplified by Christ? That way I come up with the Master's Plan and not my own master plan. When I come to a crossroads or decision that must be made, I ask in my daily quiet time, "Lord, what will you have me to do?" Then I listen, write down my impressions, and check them against my ultimate goals. Though this is not a foolproof method, it is a way of getting in touch with your God-given dream.

Organize Your Week

Once you know your priorities, or the direction God intends for your life, it is much easier to put your daily life into order. By following my friend Mary Ann's advice to organize my week each Sunday afternoon, I discovered that the greatest benefit is that it brings the future into the present and makes it manageable. There is nothing magical about doing this on Sunday. Any other day will work as well. I like Sunday because it is the first day of a new week. When I organize my week, I don't write down routine things that have to be done each day, such as making beds and washing dishes. I do, however, think through what I want to accomplish each day and the things that have to be done to make that possible.

If, for example, I have a speaking engagement on

Thursday, I schedule time during the week for preparation—for reading and thinking, writing the speech, and studying it—so that I can deliver it confidently and without notes. If the patio furniture needs to be cleaned on Friday, I determine on Sunday afternoon what cleaning materials need to be purchased and include that with my grocery list. I also have learned that if I can coordinate errands, I can save large blocks of time for creative work. On the way to the grocery store, I can pick up the dry cleaning and leave shoes at the shoe-repair shop. Not only do I save gas, but I also save lots of wear and tear on my disposition.

One of the most helpful things I do when I organize my week is to decide what I will wear each day. If the weather changes drastically, then I make last-minute changes in my wardrobe choice. Knowing what you are going to wear each day of the week eliminates indecision or wearing the same thing three days in a row. The latter might be okay if you are working around the house—though a change of clothes gives us a lift in spirit—but obviously it is not okay if you are in a business or professional setting. As part of my weekly planning, I check everything before I put it away to be sure there isn't a loose button or a spot to be cleaned before the next wearing.

Through the years my children often have teased me about my "everlasting lists"—on the bulletin board for chores; on the desk for telephone calls; on my calendar for engagements, birthdays, and things to be done this week and month. I have sometimes thought that if I lost my calendar I would be disoriented for a year!

Though planning for the week is fairly easy for me, this will seem restrictive for others. You may want to plan each evening for the following day. Or you may be one of those rare persons who can keep priorities in your mind, see clearly what needs to be done, and plan as you go. No one method is right.

Organizing Ideas

1. As you plan your week, begin by asking: In keeping with my life goals, what do I most want to accomplish this week? Be sure those three or four things are part of your planning, even if you have to eliminate some things that may seem urgent but are not important.

2. By midweek, check your list and ask: How am I doing? If you have had some interruptions—unexpected company, a sick child, a new assignment at work—you may have to change your game plan. Don't be discouraged. Simply ask: In light of this new development, what is most important to do?

3. Write your daily "to do" lists in a daily planner or small notebook you can carry with you. At the beginning of the day, take a quick look at the list to get a clear direction.

4. Begin each day by asking: Lord, what do you want me to do today?

Plan for Interruptions

No matter what method we use, we should stay flexible and allow time for spontaneity. At times married couples need nothing more than to drop scheduled activities and have an evening out or a weekend away. Likewise, children need to experience times when parents can drop everything and go on a picnic. We also need to plan for interruptions. Remember that the point of being organized is not to become *efficient* but to become *effective*. We *can* become spontaneous, learn to enjoy our families, and pursue our dreams. There will be days, however, when everything has to be set aside for a crisis or for the needs of a family member or a friend.

An important part of planning for interruptions is having a picture of the kind of family we want to be—whether yours is a single-parent, two-parent, or blended family. This helps us to keep our priorities in focus and adapt appropriately when interruptions come. Dr. Stephen Covey suggests in his book *Seven Habits of Highly Effective People* that every family write a mission statement. He gives several examples and suggests that all the children who are living at home participate. Parents, then, are to keep the mission statement firmly in their minds and communicate it regularly to their children. For example, "In our family, we stand for honesty and fairness." If a parent regularly reviews the mission statement in his or her mind, it will permeate the subconscious mind with amazing results. This necessitates our staying close to Christ—not only to ensure that our picture is in keeping with his purposes, but also to be encouraged and empowered to realize the dream, even when interruptions disrupt our lives.

Begin and End the Day with God

The best way to make the most of our days, to "prioritize and organize" our lives, is daily prayer. Prayer enables us to have insight into where we have been and where God wants us to go. In such a quiet time recently, I reviewed my goals for the past fifteen years. I could honestly pray the prayer of Gert Behanna: "I ain't what I ought to be and I ain't what I'm going to be; but, thank God, I ain't what I used to be!"

In the introduction to this book, I spoke of the importance of beginning the day with God by conditioning our minds with Scripture before we even get out of bed. This might include verses such as these: "This is the day which the LORD hath made; [I] will rejoice and be glad in it" (Psalm 118:24); "Trust in the LORD with all thine heart; and lean not unto thine own understanding. In all thy ways acknowledge him, and he shall direct thy paths" (Proverbs 3:5-6); "I can do all things through Christ who strengthens me" (Philippians 4:13 NKJV). If we follow this conditioning with a quiet time in which we read devotional material and pray, we will "set our sails" for the day.

I have discovered it equally important to spend the last waking minutes of the day turning loose of my worries and stresses. As I take off my clothes, I think symbolically of taking off my concerns and leaving them with God for the evening. Then I give thanks for his presence in the day that is ending, adding, "I have done the best I could today, Lord; forgive my mistakes and failures. Now I ask you to take the night shift." Following that I say silently this scriptural promise: "He gives His beloved sleep" (Psalm 127:2 NKJV).

Psychologists tell us that our thoughts just before we go to sleep will determine the quality of our sleep, including our dreams. When we have done our best to prioritize and organize our days according to God's plan and direction for our lives, we are more prone to sleep soundly and peacefully and awaken refreshed and ready for the new day.

Steps for Prioritizing and Organizing

1. Remember that time is limited, so you need to enjoy and appreciate the current season of your life, daily seeking God's guidance.

2. Don't procrastinate. When you are decisive and meet your goals, you have a sense of accomplishment, of being in control.

3. Learn to say "no" without feeling guilty. To do this means keeping your priorities clearly in focus.

4. Thoughtfully and prayerfully determine your three to five life goals.

5. At the beginning of each week, organize your week by writing down things you hope to accomplish each day. Otherwise, time is wasted on trivial matters or what may only seem urgent.

6. Plan to consolidate your errands. If you are going to the grocery store or to take a child to an after-school activity, think of the other stops you can make en route to save time, gas, and lots of wear and tear on your disposition.

7. Plan your wardrobe for the week.

8. Begin and end each day with God. Begin the day with rejocing and anticipation and a request for guidance. End each day with thanksgiving.

9. Live each day with joy and trust. "Trust in the LORD with all thine heart; and lean not unto thine own understanding. In all thy ways acknowledge him, and he shall direct thy paths" (Proverbs 3:5-6).

II.

Look

5.

ASK YOURSELF, "LORD, WHAT DO YOU WANT ME TO DO?"

It happened when I was only ten years old, but I remember it as if it were yesterday. I was traveling with my parents and younger brother from our home in North Carolina for a weekend visit with an aunt in Georgia. Because we got a later start than we had anticipated, we were driving after dark for most of the trip. It was an Alfred Hitchcock kind of night—rainy, foggy, and windy, with black clouds covering the stars and moon so that you could hardly see your hand in front of your face.

Suddenly we came to road construction. It was necessary to take a detour down a country road that was as bumpy as an old-fashioned washboard. After less than a mile on that road, we came to a crossroads. The detour sign had blown over and was lying in the middle of the road. We had no idea which way to go, and there wasn't another car in sight. My father was a man of great intuition and deep faith. He stopped the car, had a prayer for guidance, and then proceeded down the "road less traveled." My brother and I insisted that we should take the road that looked to have had more recent travelers. Fortunately for all of us, my father was right. We were soon on the main road and nearing our destination.

In my adult life I have frequently thought of that incident, and I have realized that life is full of crossroads—choosing a vocation, a marriage partner, a job, a house, a church; deciding which way to go when our lives have been turned upside down by an earthquake, a life-threatening illness, the death of a loved one, divorce, financial failure, or any of the experiences that can traumatize us.

Preparing for these life-shaping crossroads means that we constantly work at deepening our spiritual roots. My father's favorite Scripture passage was Proverbs 3:5-6: "Trust in the LORD with all thine heart; and lean not unto thine own understanding. In all thy ways acknowledge him, and he shall direct thy paths." The people who handle crossroads decisions best are those who consistently seek to live in God's will and purpose. The question that Paul asked following his Damascus Road conversion should be the question we ask at all of life's crossroads, both small and large: "Lord, what do You want me to do?" (Acts 9:6 NKJV).

How Do We Discover God's Will?

God makes his will known in many ways. Some of these are independent of our efforts—such as circumstances, a chance conversation, or a line from a book that speaks a message when we are not thinking about or seeking guidance. Other times we receive guidance when we actively seek it through prayer, Bible study, or counsel with a trusted friend. Sometimes it comes through intuition—a strong inner feeling that this is the right path. I have found it helpful to look objectively at what I perceive to be guidance by writing down pros and cons. This gives the balance of logic to what could be my own wishful thinking. Adding my best thinking to my perceived guidance, I slowly come to an inner sense of "knowing." If I still lack the assurance of "knowing" and need to make a decision, I go with my best judgment. I'm convinced that God honors our desire to do his will and sends the Holy Spirit to inspire our minds.

Five Ways We Discover God's Will

1. Prayer
2. Scripture
3. Intuition
4. Our Reasoned Thinking
5. Circumstances and People

1. Prayer

One of the first and best ways to receive God's guidance is through prayer. Because praying for guidance was part of my father's everyday life, it was only natural that at a crossroads crisis he stopped the car and prayed for direction. Praying at a crossroads crisis is more difficult if we want to control all the events and people of our lives, or if we are accustomed to simply doing what comes next without a thought about the purposes of God. Sometimes we don't want to know what God wishes us to do.

Once I worked in an office where there was an extremely efficient executive secretary. She was a pleasant woman in her fifties who had never married. Her job seemed to be her life. She was at the office early and often worked late. Most of us expected her to be in her job until her retirement.

Then one day she walked into the office and announced the unthinkable: She was to be married in two weeks and would move out of town. A sales representative had come to town on business, had given "Miss Maude" (a Southern term of respect given her by younger members of the staff) a "big rush," and had proposed to her. Our employer was stunned by the news. Being a very religious man, his immediate response was, "Maude, don't make such a big decision so quickly. Let's pray about it." Quick as a flash she replied, "Don't you dare!" Obviously "Miss Maude" had wanted to be married for a long time, and this was her first opportunity. Unfortunately, she should have listened to our employer. In six months she was back at work in the office. Her prince charming turned out to be a first-class con man who absconded with all her life's savings and fled the country. Sometimes we are too preoccupied or too rebellious to seek God's direction, and we suffer the consequences.

Our lives are so full of activities, so cluttered with trivial pursuits, so preoccupied with the "nitty-gritty" of daily living that God can't get through our chronic busyness. Our devotional lives must include some silence and listening for God's direction. My own experience is that this isn't easy. As with most of us today, my system seems to be set on "go and do" rather than "sit and listen." It is a consciously disciplined effort to "sit and listen," because skill in listening comes only through practice. My own process is (1) read from the Bible and/or other devotional material; (2) think (about what I have read); (3) pray (including praise, thanksgiving, intercession, and specific requests for guidance); and (4) silence (during which ideas will pop into my mind). Some of the thoughts that come to me during this period of silence are creative ideas that will have direct bearing on the decision I need to make. The Bible is full of passages emphasizing the importance of quiet listening for God. Two of my favorites are "In quietness and in confidence shall be your strength" (Isaiah 30:15) and "Be still, and know that I am God" (Psalm 46:10).

Jesus demonstrated the importance of prayer by his own example. In addition to regular participation in corporate worship—"As his custom was, he went into the synagogue" (Luke 4:16)—Jesus drew apart from the crowds and from his preaching and healing to be reenergized and to receive God's direction. Always this was his practice when he faced momentous decisions, such as when he spent forty days in the wilderness fasting and praying about the direction his ministry should take.

Later, when he recognized the probable cost of his ministry and felt the need of affirmation, he went to the Mount of Transfiguration with Peter, James, and John (see Matthew 17:1-9). On the mountain he was transfigured before them. "His face did shine as the sun, and his raiment was white as the light" (v. 2), and they heard a voice from heaven saying, "This is my beloved Son, in whom I am well pleased" (v. 5).

Perhaps the incident we remember most vividly was following the Last Supper, when the Crucifixion loomed large before him and he withdrew alone in the Garden of Gethsemane. He wrestled with the fears and the dread of facing the Cross until he received the strength to say, "Nevertheless not what I will, but what thou wilt" (Mark 14:36).

If Jesus had not habitually gone apart to pray and listen, he would not have been conditioned to seek guidance at the big crossroads. Prayer, then, is the first and perhaps most important means of seeking guidance.

2. Scripture

Another way to discover God's guidance is through Scripture. The more we study God's Word, the more we know what he wants of us: holiness, joyful obedience, and service to others in his name. It is amazing how in my daily Bible reading, a passage seems to leap out at me, often with an answer to the very problem with which I am struggling. Though I don't believe in Bible bingo (opening the Bible, pointing your finger to a passage, and expecting it to guide you), I sometimes have turned to a different book from the one in which I was currently spending time and, in the reading, have found a new insight. It can also be helpful to read a particular passage from various Bible translations.

Regular Bible reading is the secret to allowing us to see the ways in which God has worked out his purposes through the centuries. In particular, reading from the New Testament with some regularity allows us to saturate ourselves with the spirit of Christ. This practice helps us find verses that speak directly to a problem we may be having, without pulling a verse out of context to support our own belief or desire.

3. Intuition

Though most of our consistent guidance will come through God's Word and prayer, God also guides through intuition. A friend of mine, Lucy McElhaney, had such an experience. Houseguests had left in the late afternoon, and she had taken sheets and towels from the guest room and put them into the washing machine around 9:00 P.M. When she was ready to place the sheets in the dryer, she heard an inner voice saying, *Hang them on the clothesline.* Then she said to herself, *That's a crazy thought. I haven't hung clothes outside for years.*

As she placed the sheets in the dryer, the inner voice became compelling and authoritative: *Hang the sheets outside.* Still arguing, she found herself thinking, *But it is 9:00 at night. Those sheets won't dry before they become damp again with the morning dew.* Yet, even as she argued, she was taking the sheets out of the dryer and heading for the clothesline. Never had she had such a clear and insistent experience of guidance. It was a little frightening.

Once outside, she heard it. The cry was frail and weak, but it was a call for help. "Help, help! Someone help me, please!" After rushing back into the house, Lucy asked her husband, Bob, to help her determine the direction of the call. They jumped into their car and cruised the neighborhood until they found Mr. Hornaday, an eighty-two-year-old member of their church. His wife had died only months earlier, and he lived alone. That evening he had been carrying two bags of garbage down a long flight of steps leading to the backyard, and he hadn't been able to catch himself when he stumbled. When Lucy and Bob found him, he was lying at the bottom of the steps, unable to move because of two broken legs. For forty-five minutes he had been calling for help, but, insulated by air-conditioning and closed doors, the neighbors had not heard. Only the one who had trained herself to listen for God's voice could respond to the emergency.

4. Our Reasoned Thinking

Ruth Stafford Peale once said in a speech that when she had a big decision to make, she tried to think about options, talk them over with her husband, and then write down pros and cons. When she went into her prayer time, she envisioned Christ sitting across from her as she stated the problem and her request for guidance. Then, in the silence, she would receive a strong and intuitive feeling of one option being preferable over the others. She said that on rare occasions when she received no strong feeling and had a deadline for decision making, she looked over her carefully thought-through pros and cons and went with her most reasoned thinking, believing that the Holy Spirit was guiding her in the process.

I have found reasoned thinking to be most helpful when a decision impinges on others, particularly family members. For example, if I receive an invitation to speak out of town, I need to check my husband's schedule for those days. Are there church, business, or social occasions we need to attend together? How important are they? How does he feel about my being away? Is there a family birthday or other event during that time? Since my husband and I host a family dinner to celebrate each birthday in the family, that event is very significant, though the dinner doesn't always have to be held on the exact day. Am I needed to keep grandchildren if our son or daughter-in-law is away? All these things need to be considered as I make a decision. You will have your own list of questions that must be considered. Only after you have given careful thought to these questions are you ready to begin the three-step process of exploring options, listing pros and cons, and praying.

5. Circumstances and People

My own experience is that God often guides us through circumstances and people, including those shared with us through books and sermons. The late Catherine Marshall tells in her book *Something More* about receiving specific guidance from an unexpected source. While writing the book *A Man Called Peter*, she needed some material about Peter Marshall's stepfather, Peter Findlay, who had lived in Scotland. She said that Peter Findlay had died a few years earlier, and that "Mother Janet" simply didn't remember those details. Then one evening she and her son were invited to dinner at the home of new friends in Washington, D.C. During the course of the dinner, she felt a strong urge to tell about the needed information. She had hardly begun when the host asked, "Do you mean Peter Findlay?" The air became electric with excitement as she replied, "Yes, why? Did you know him?" Smiling broadly, the host replied, "I worked beside him for six years during that period." She writes that it was a safe guess that out of the 800,000 residents in the District of Columbia, this was the only person who had the material she needed.

In less dramatic and direct ways, people have given me God's guidance through their faithful discipleship. For example, a friend who remained cheerful and loving during long years of her husband's debilitating illness helped me to see how I could be a witness for Christ during the six years that my father, ill with emphysema, lived in our home. My friend's wisdom in getting needed help and planning for her own personal renewal also served as guidance for me.

So God guides us in myriad and wonderful ways. We can be sure that God loves us—"We love him, because he first loved us" (1 John 4:19); that he is with us constantly in the person of the Holy Spirit—"Lo, I am with you always, even to the end of the age" (Matthew 28:20 NKJV); and that he wants to guide us—"Trust in the LORD with all thine heart; and lean not unto thine own understanding. In all thy ways acknowledge him, and he shall direct thy paths" (Proverbs 3:5-7).

Steps for Discovering God's Will

1. Learn to look for and recognize the crossroads in life. At different times in your life, you may find yourself at a crossroads in your career, marriage, family relationships, or friendships. Or a crossroads may be a physical, mental, or spiritual challenge. Rather than habitually doing whatever comes next, be open to the possibility that your life may need to go in a different direction.

2. Stop in the midst of your chronic busyness to ask the question that Paul asked after his Damascus Road experience: "Lord, what do You want me to do?" (Acts 9:6 NKJV). Sometimes we go pell-mell on our way without asking the question because we are preoccupied or rebellious. We don't want to know the answer. If there is an area of your life in which you are reluctant to seek God's will, this is the area you need to surrender to God. Remember that what he wills for us is for our highest good.

3. Listen for God's answer, God's direction, remembering that God guides through prayer, Scripture, intuition, reasoned thinking, circumstances, and people.

4. Trust in God's never-failing presence and love and God's willingness to direct your path.

6.

LOOKING BACK ENABLES YOU TO FACE FORWARD

"Nell, this is Anne. I am in town for a meeting today, and I wondered if you would join me at my hotel for lunch."

"Absolutely," I replied. "I'll have to do a little rearranging, but I will be there at noon." On the way to the hotel, I thought about Anne. She had been in high school and college when my husband served as pastor of her church in another city. Anne was attractive, vivacious, and fun-loving. Her only obvious fault was an unharnessed temper—and thereby hangs the tale.

During most of the years we had known her, she had dated Hal, a level-headed young man who was studying engineering. Anne's anger caused the couple to break up on a regular basis, but soon they would be together again. Then two months before graduation, Anne became furious over a minor incident and told Hal that she never wanted to see him again. He took her at her word, and four months later he was married to someone else.

Anne was devastated. Each time I had seen her in the intervening years, she had told me the story with intense feeling. As I drove to the hotel, I wondered if she would rehearse the incident again. I didn't have to wonder long. No sooner had we put napkins in our laps than she began.

Looking her straight in the eye, I asked, "Anne, how long ago did that happen?"

"Oh well, if you don't want to hear it. . . ." she replied.

I persisted, "That has nothing to do with the question. How long ago did it happen?"

"Ten years ago," she said quietly.

Reaching across the table, I took her hand and said as gently as I could, "Anne, don't you see what has happened? You have been living in the past. You have wasted ten wonderful years in your life, and God wants you to move on."

Quickly she changed the subject, and the rest of the luncheon conversation was on a superficial basis. But six months later I received the following note: "Dear Nell, when you made me confront my situation last fall, I was angry and resentful. Soon, however, I began to see the logic of your statement, and I want you to know that Dan and I have been dating for three months and will be married in the fall. We would like to have you and Ralph present for the wedding and seated with the family. Love, Anne."

I smiled as I placed that special letter on my desk. *How wonderful!* I thought. Then came another thought: *But she could have done this ten years ago!*

Everyone knows we shouldn't live in the past. It is a wonderful place to visit—to be encouraged by past memories and to learn from past mistakes. But if we try to live there, we waste the energy—physical, mental, and spiritual—that is needed to live today with zest and effectiveness. We also forget our potential for the future when we put our lives on hold.

Living in the Past Can Be Addictive

Living in the past can become as addictive as a drug or as watching television, which is itself a kind of plug-in drug. This addiction allows people to evade responsibility and to live on the sidelines of life. Are there other payoffs for a person who insists on reliving past tragedies? Much wanted attention and sympathy are the only ones I can think of, but they always deny us the quality of abundant life that Jesus promised (see John 10:10).

The Bible has many stories of people seeking to live in the past. In Genesis 19:1-28, we read that God saved Lot and his wife and two daughters from the destruction of Sodom. God told them not to look back. Lot obeyed, because he was glad to be out of Sodom. But Lot's wife, addicted to her memories, looked back and turned into a pillar of salt. Obviously, we won't turn into a pillar of salt when we live in the past, but we may turn a deaf ear to God calling us to move into his future.

Years later, when the children of Israel were making their trek through the wilderness en route to the Promised Land, God provided "manna" for their daily bread supply. Some of them tried to hold on to yesterday's allotment only to discover that it had spoiled and they had none for today (see Exodus 16:14-21). Likewise, when we hold on to the past, we dissipate the energy, time, and creative imagination needed for living today and leaning forward into God's tomorrow.

Recently a man told me that he put his life on hold while he relived the memories of past football glory. Though he had a job, he performed the task only in a perfunctory manner. Instead of using his creativity to grow professionally and personally, he daydreamed about touchdowns he had made years before amid thundering applause. It was only when he lost his job that he was jolted into reality and forced to face himself and to recognize the tragic waste of nine years. He started over with a new commitment to Christ and a new commitment to live in the "now." The daily affirmation he chose was Psalm 118:24: "This is the day the LORD has made; let us rejoice and be glad in it" (NIV). Recently I asked the daughter of a one-hundred-year-old woman what caused her mother to be so contemporary and positive. Her reply was this: "She daily says, believes in, and lives by Psalm 118:24."

God Calls Us Forward

Over and over the Bible encourages us not to bog down in yesterday but to live today and to move with God into the future. Is this a paradox? Is it impossible to live fully today and move into the future? I don't think so. As we seek to live in the spirit of Christ today, we can be aware of the nudges and opportunities to envision God's future and to initiate the necessary changes. The key, of course, is complete trust in God.

One of the most vivid examples of this is God's command to the children of Israel at the decisive moment when they stood before the deep and swirling waters of the Red Sea. They were afraid of being drowned as they stepped into the waters, and equally afraid of the Pharaoh, whose chariots were in hot pursuit of them. At that decisive moment, God spoke to Moses: "Speak unto the children of Israel, that they go forward" (Exodus 14:15). It is important to note that they were commanded to go forward *before* the waters parted. They had to step out in faith, trusting the faithfulness of God.

Know When to Look Back

Sometimes we need to remember the faithfulness of God in the past to give us courage to move forward. At those times, we stop and look back to learn from our mistakes and to recall God's enduring faithfulness. Two logical times each year to do this are on our birthdays and at the beginning of a new calendar year. At those times we can evaluate where we have been in order to determine how to move on from here. Carl Sandburg once wrote that we should never record today in our diaries what happened today, because it takes time to understand what *really* has happened today.

Looking back instead of living in the past is accomplished through short visits when we seek to understand our present by seeing clearly the patterns of our past. I have discovered that time seems to give objectivity in this regard. Such visits enable us to evaluate where we are at the present and move forward realistically into the future. Obviously, it is much easier to see life retrospectively, since most of us have 20/20 hindsight. Benjamin Franklin once declared that there are three hard things: steel, diamonds, and knowing yourself. I've learned that it is easier to unmask and see the real person as we study patterns of our lives, a part of which is seeing the past clearly.

Recently I had a birthday, though I am not telling you which one it was. Mary Kay Ashe, the cosmetic executive, was right when she said, "A woman who will tell her age will tell anything!" Amid the celebrations with family and friends, I took time in the early morning of my birthday to look back and be grateful. A large part of my gratitude was the way in which God has guided my life. Since I normally write my prayers anyway, it was not hard on my birthday to write three other segments: things I have learned this year, my strengths and weaknesses, and my dreams for the future. That exercise, combined with my prayers of gratitude, enabled me to stand like Janus, the mythical Greek god, who could look in both directions at once; I evaluated my past as I leaned forward into the future.

One reason it was easy for me to take a quick sentimental journey into my past was that I spent two days of my birthday week at a beautiful retreat located in the mountains of North Carolina where year-round spiritual enrichment programs are held. En route to the meeting, I suddenly realized that my spiritual roots were in that place. As a young teenager at church camp, I came to faith in Christ. A camp counselor with joyous faith helped to bring me to that decision. Only a few years later, while attending a senior high youth assembly at that beautiful mountain retreat, I heard and responded to a call to full-time service in the church.

It was again on those grounds where my husband and I, after college and graduate school, did much of our courting. Recently I told him laughingly that one day while we were walking near the lake at that assembly ground, I decided he was going to be my husband. He didn't come to that decision until several months later—and through the years he has thought the engagement was all his idea!

When I look retrospectively at my life, God's faithfulness is crystal clear. Even when I have made dumb mistakes or failed or let my ego get in the driver's seat, God hasn't given up on me but has continued to work to make me whole. When I feel discouraged about my lack of motivation or my ineffectiveness, I affirm Philippians 1:6: "He who has begun a good work in you will complete it" (NKJV).

English author Francis Thompson speaks of God as the "Hound of Heaven," who forever seeks and pursues us. As a young man he wanted to enter the Roman Catholic priesthood but was turned down because of his timidity and a nervous condition. He tried becoming a doctor but failed in that. Then he tried to enlist in the army, but he was turned down because he couldn't pass the physical examination. Depressed from his failures, he began to smoke opium and became addicted. It was through the help of a Christian couple that he gave up opium, came back to faith, and began to use his God-given talents for creative writing. In his famous poem "The Hound of Heaven," he tells how he fled from God and how God never gave up on him:

I fled Him, down the nights and down the days;
  I fled Him down the arches of the years;
And down the labyrinthine ways
Of my own mind; and in the mist of tears
I hid from Him, and under running laughter. . . .
  Still with unhurrying chase
And unperturbèd pace,
Deliberate speed, majestic instancy,
  Came on the following feat,
  And a Voice above there beat—
"Naught shelters thee, who wilt not shelter Me."

Look Toward the Future

As I look toward the future, I realize that not a single one of us knows what our future holds; but we do know who holds the future. As Browning said in his poem "Rabbi Ben Ezra," "Our times are in His hands."

During my birthday evaluation, I realized anew that if I want to participate daily in Jesus' promise of abundant living, there are certain things I must do as long as I am physically and mentally able. I invite you to choose your own expectations and commitment, or to join me in the following:

1. I will greet each new day as a gift. Upon awakening, I will "set my sails" for the day by affirming Psalm 118:24: "This is the day which the LORD has made; [I] will rejoice and be glad in it."

2. I will have planned and organized my day before I am catapulted into it, because I know that time is of the essence and should not be trivialized. As Stephen Covey said in his book *First Things First*, "Anything less than a conscious commitment to the important is an unconscious commitment to the unimportant." I will try to keep the main thing the main thing. Already I have learned that it is easier to say "no" if there is a "yes" burning inside me.

3. I will try to stay flexible, knowing that people are more important than things or agendas. The kingdom of God is the kingdom of relationships. Next in importance to my relationship with God through Christ is my relationship with my family, and I will always make time for it. As author Elton Trueblood has said, "The family is the kingdom of God in miniature."

4. I will continue, as long as I have breath, to allow whatever talents I have to be used in service to others, for the sake of Christ. Knowing that God expects us to replenish our energies for service, I will take time to relax, laugh, pray, and enjoy the beauty of the world and the beauty in people.

5. I will strive to live each day so that at my life's end, I can say that I have done my best to do God's will.

If you want to move ahead with God, you must learn from the past, live fully today, face forward, and trust God for the future. Continue to recall with gratitude that God is at work, molding you into the likeness of Christ. And finally, remember that because of God's faithfulness in the past, you can move into the future with confidence, great expectations, and joyful anticipation that "He who has begun a good work in you will complete it" (Philippians 1:6 NKJV).

Steps for Moving Ahead with God

1. Learn from your past; don't live in it. Let go of past mistakes and look for the possibilities in God's today.

2. Take time to look back at your life periodically in order to recall God's faithfulness to you. Write down the ways in which he has guided your life. Who are the people who have helped direct your faith journey? Write down their names and give thanks for each one.

3. Greet each new day as a gift.

4. Organize your day before it begins.

5. Stay flexible.

6. Use your talents in service to others in the name of Christ.

7. Begin to see yourself as God would have you to become in the future. Ask yourself, "In order to participate daily in Jesus' promise of abundant living, what three or more things will I commit to do as long as I am physically and mentally able?"

8. Live each day so that one day you may affirm with Paul: "I have fought a good fight, I have finished my course, I have kept the faith" (2 Timothy 4:7).

7.

LOOK FOR GOD'S OPTIONS

She was only nineteen. Life should have been full of myriad choices and exciting possibilities. Instead, her face reflected the resignation that one often sees in the eyes of nursing home residents. She was seated across the aisle from me on a small commuter plane on a hot summer afternoon. Then her tears began to flow—first as if from a slow faucet, and then with the torrent of a gusher.

"Is there anything I can do to help?" I asked cautiously, realizing that the young woman was on the verge of hysteria. When she could compose herself, she told me a terrible story of degradation. At fourteen she had run away from an abusive and uncaring home situation in the city to which we were flying. In the five years she had been away, her parents had made no attempt to locate her. Once in her new town, she had seen a former schoolmate who reported that her parents had simply said "good riddance" after her disappearance.

Feeling unloved and afraid, she tried desperately to find jobs so that she could support herself, but with limited education and no job skills, no good job came her way. She was able to find a few short-term, menial-type jobs, but the money provided only the barest necessities.

Then one day a short, overweight, middle-aged man

named Jim came into the fast-food restaurant where she worked. Recognizing her vulnerability, he invited her to go out to dinner with him. That was the first time since she had left home six months earlier that anyone had shown any concern for her. He executed his plan for her with the smooth strategy of an undercover agent. Convinced that he really loved her, she moved into his palatial home. Only then did she discover the truth. She was one of a stable of young girls whose bodies were used to make money for Jim and his "empire."

The girls were locked in the mansion and were never allowed to leave the tightly secured grounds. Her only remuneration was room and board, and the opportunity to see an occasional in-house movie. On two occasions she tried to escape, but she was apprehended, punished, and made to endure unspeakable indignities. Her spirit began to die within her. Little by little, despair was overtaking her mind, and her body as well.

Seeing what was happening and not wishing to have her death on his hands, one of the guards offered to help her escape and to buy a one-way airline ticket to her hometown. It was a risky plan, but it had worked. Elaine, who had just turned nineteen, was heading home. Two options faced her there: a family that did not want her, and the likelihood that Jim would find her and return her to his prison. It wasn't surprising, then, that she ended her sordid tale with these words: "There is no hope."

Quickly I replied: "Oh, but you are wrong there. God hasn't moved away from you. You have moved away from him. He is right here with us now. That's what Christ came to tell us. All you have to do, in repentance, is to reach out and accept the marvelous gift of love and forgiveness and salvation." We talked for a while about this gift that seemed to her too good to be true. Then we had a prayer, and I gave her the name of a minister to contact in that town. When we got off the plane, an amazing thing happened. As I gave her a good-bye hug, she said, "May I show you something?" She opened her purse, took out a suicide note, and said, "I was planning to take my life today, but you gave me hope." I didn't give her hope. God gave her hope, but I was available to point out some of his options for her lonely, miserable life. After she committed her life to Christ, she needed to become a part of the church, the Body of Christ. There she could find acceptance, love, and support as she began a new life-style.

Since that day I have become increasingly aware that life is full of dead-end streets. Our situation may not be as desperate as the young woman's on the plane, but there are times when we feel hopeless. It could be a job that is headed nowhere or has suddenly ended, a marriage that is on the rocks, a terminal illness, a relationship with a rebellious child or difficult person, unmerited criticism, financial reverses, or number of other things.

If we are to master the art of "being up on down days," we need to look continually for God's options for ourselves, as well as help others to find them. The Bible recommends a four-letter word, *hope*, as an indispensable part of our spiritual equipment.

Hope: Our Spiritual Equipment

The tests were completed; the surgery was scheduled. Now I was waiting in my hospital room for the doctor to come by with final instructions. There was apprehension in my heart as I waited. The tests had indicated that a large ovarian tumor was pushing against other organs of my body and must be removed. What we didn't know was whether there was a malignancy.

When the doctor walked into my hospital room, some of my anxieties subsided. His very presence brought assurance. His competency as a gynecologist and oncologist was recognized far and wide. Even his voice seemed to say that whatever happened, everything was going to be all right.

I relaxed as he told me what to expect the following day—from the kind of anesthesia to be used to his options when he saw the tumor. If the tumor seemed to be self-contained and the immediate pathology report looked good, then I would be in surgery less than two hours and would return to my hospital room. If the tumor proved to be malignant and the cancer had spread to other organs, I would be in surgery longer and then would be taken to the intensive care unit.

The following day when I began to awaken from the anesthetic, it was obvious that I was not in my hospital room. Nurses were hovering, and I could hear the sound of life-sustaining machines. The clock on the wall told me that it had been eight hours since I had been wheeled into the surgery suite. I seemed to have tubes coming out of every organ of my body. My heart sank. Hope vanished. Yet momentarily, when my vision cleared, I could see my husband and son standing on one side of my bed and my doctor on the other side. They were smiling.

In a strong, confident voice, the doctor said: "There was a malignancy, but I think we were able to get it all. As a precaution, however, you will have nine or ten months of chemotherapy, and then we will have a second-look surgery. I am sure you are going to be fine." My heart began to soar.

Webster defines *hope* as "a feeling of desire accompanied by anticipation and expectation." The desire to be well had been there all along, but it became hope when the doctor gave me reason to anticipate. Hope for me that day was a light, bouyant feeling that enabled me to sing, despite pain and tubes and the prospect of chemotherapy. Running through my mind were the words of the song "Cockeyed Optimist" from the Broadway musical "South Pacific": "I am stuck like a dope with a thing called hope and I can't get it out of my mind." The lyricist for that upbeat musical once said, "I just couldn't write anything without hope in it."

God is incapable of writing anything without hope in it. His work is full of hope. The biblical understanding of hope is far more than wishful thinking. It is substantive, strong, and eternal. Hebrews 6:19 reminds us that our hope is "a strong and trustworthy anchor for our souls, connecting us with God himself behind the sacred curtains of heaven" (TLB).

That beloved and often quoted thirteenth chapter of 1 Corinthians names three powerful weapons for living fully and joyfully: "And now abide faith, hope, love, these three; but the greatest of these is love" (v. 13 NKJV). In order to look for God's options, we need to understand the power of hope in helping us to see the way out.

The Power of Hope

When we lose hope, we stop trying. In 1950, Florence Chadwick set a new women's speed record for swimming the English Channel. Later her goal was to swim from Catalina Island to Los Angeles. On the morning of the race, the weather was cold and the smog was so thick you could almost cut it with a knife. To make matters worse, a killer whale had been spotted swimming in those very waters. The combination of cold, smog, and fear depleted Chadwick's supply of hope.

Her mother and her trainer rode in the rescue boat alongside her. They encouraged her with words and a warm drink when she looked as if she might be coming out of the water. Finally, even their encouragement didn't persuade her to continue. She didn't complete the race. Imagine her surprise when she learned that she gave up less than one-fourth mile from the Los Angeles shoreline.

She commented that if only she could have seen the shoreline, she wouldn't have lost hope. The following year she completed the swim in record time. She told reporters that she kept her hope by always seeing the shoreline in her mind.

Paul wrote: "For in hope we were saved. Now hope that is seen is not hope. For who hopes for what is seen?" (Romans 8:24 NRSV). Those words never rang more true to me than when I read a newspaper article several years ago about a man caught in a sudden snow blizzard in the Midwest. The man's car stalled several miles from his home, so he began walking. The snow was falling so heavily and the winds were gusting with such force that the man became disoriented; he must have felt he was hopelessly lost. The following morning his frozen body was found only a few hundred feet from his home. If only he had kept on walking in hope for a few more minutes, his life might have been saved.

Do you ever wonder how many troubled marriages could be saved if, in hope, the partners keep on trying, or what breakthroughs in science might be possible if hope is not lost? Surely it was the power of hope that kept Thomas A. Edison going when hundreds of experiments to produce an electric lightbulb failed. Before his breakthrough, a young reporter asked the famous scientist if he was discouraged by all the failures. "These haven't been failures," replied Edison, "we have simply found 999 ways not to produce an electric lightbulb."

Through the years, leaders in almost every human endeavor have affirmed the value and potency of hope. In *Walden,* Henry David Thoreau suggested that hope helps us to grasp the future. He wrote: "I learned this . . . by my experiment: that if one advances confidently in the direction of his dreams and endeavors to live that life which he has imagined, he will meet with a success unexpected in common hours."

Recently I read an excerpt of an article about hope written by Daniel Goldman for the *New York Times.* It was titled "Hope Emerges as Key to Success in Life." Goldman wrote: "Psychologists are finding that hope plays a surprisingly potent role in giving people a measurable advantage in areas as diverse as academic achievement, working in difficult jobs, and coping with tragedy."

That quotation reminded me of an article in our local newspaper about a college student who was doing miserably during the first quarter of his freshman year. His adviser called him in to say: "What has happened to you? You were a straight A student in high school, yet here you are making D's. What's the problem?"

"I don't have the IQ to do college work," the freshman answered.

"How do you know that?" asked the adviser.

"I saw the results of my test," replied the young student.

When the student described the test, the advisor said: "That wasn't an IQ test. That test indicated that you were in the 95th percentile of all college freshmen. You are brilliant!" From that point on, the boy's grades soared. It was the power of hope that made the difference.

By regularly reading God's Word; by keeping our daily walk with Christ vital through prayer; by regular worship; by association with positive Christians, we can cultivate and hold on to hope. And what a powerful difference it can make in our lives!

With God Is Our Best Hope

My husband and I have had the privilege of visiting some of the fastest-growing churches from Maine to California. The book we wrote to detail our visits is titled *Churches of Vision.* Among those interesting churches is Metropolitan United Methodist on Woodward Avenue in Detroit, Michigan.

On the lawn in front of the church is one lone statue. The story goes that the statue is the result of a sermon preached by Dr. Merton S. Rice during a time of economic recession when the attitude of hope for the future was at a premium. In the congregation of discouraged people that day was a notable artist. He was so impressed by the sensible message of undefeated faith and hope that he hurried to his studio and created the statue that now stands on the church lawn. The statue depicts a man struggling in adversity, with his muscles straining to overcome. On the base of the statue is inscribed the scripture upon which Dr. Rice's sermon was based: "Why art thou cast down, O my soul? and why art thou disquieted within me? hope thou in God: for I shall yet praise him, who is the health of my countenance, and my God" (Psalm 42:11).

When discouragement or despair seem to have a hold on us, God is our best hope. God holds us steady in times of temptation and difficulty, draws us toward his goals, strengthens our spirits when our bodies are weak, and enables us to walk confidently into the future, even into the next dimension of life.

Steps for Looking for God's Options

1. When you encounter a dead-end street in your life—related to your job, your marriage, your children, your finances, or something else—look for God's options by asking: "Lord, what do you want me to do?" Remember that nothing can happen to you that you and God cannot handle. Affirm: "With God all things are possible" (Matthew 19:26); "I can do all things through Christ who strengthens me" (Philippians 4:13 NKJV).

2. In times of difficulty, draw upon your spiritual equipment, which includes faith, hope, and love (1 Corinthians 13:13).

3. Remember that, like Florence Chadwick, you can keep going if you always "see the shoreline in your mind." Don't quit. You may be close to a breakthrough.

4. Memorize this and other Scripture verses on hope, and use them as daily affirmations during a devotional time or throughout the day as needed: "Hope is the anchor of the soul" (Hebrews 6:19, author's paraphrase).

5. Think of a time when the power of hope sustained you in a difficult situation. Relive the experience in detail. Then give thanks to God that he has given you hope as a part of your spiritual equipment for daily living.

6. Never forget that God is your best hope!

III.

Listen

8.

LISTEN TO YOUR BODY

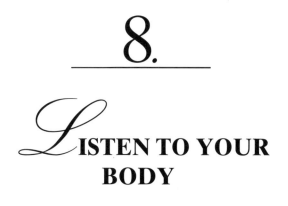

The psalmist tells us that we are complex, intricate, wonderful creations: "I will praise thee; for I am fearfully and wonderfully made" (Psalm 139:14). In Psalm 8:5 we read that we are made a little lower than the angels and that we are crowned with honor and glory. In addition, we are unique individuals. Evidence of this is that each of us has a thumb print that is different from anyone else's. That fact, in itself, is mind boggling, especially when we remember that more than five billion people live on planet Earth. Mamie McCullough, a motivational speaker from Dallas, Texas, has her seminar participants look at their thumbs and declare, "I am thumbody!" It is a reminder that we are "fearfully and wonderfully made."

Claim Your Heritage

Recognizing your uniqueness does not infer self-centeredness. You are a person of worth, not because of what you have done but because of what God has done for you through Christ. Our Christian heritage is that we are made in the image of God, redeemed by Jesus Christ, and empowered by the Holy Spirit. I am convinced that we Christians have not fully understood or claimed this heritage given us by God through Jesus Christ. In fact, as I explain in more detail in my book *Don't Put a Period Where God Put a Comma,* most of us have used only a fraction of the God-given potential within us. When we recognize that we are not the center of life—which many secular self-help books would lead us to believe—but that God is, we are on the way to becoming all that God created us to be.

Zig Ziglar, well-known author and speaker, says, "There is a God, but it is not you, and it is not me either." Only God is God; but through the death and resurrection of Christ, God has provided forgiveness and salvation and the power to become what we were created to be. "But to all who received him, who believed in his name, he gave power to become children of God" (John 1:12 NRSV). We develop confidence for living and serving as we claim this heritage.

Millions of people have been helped to claim their Christian heritage and realize their potential through the speeches and books of the late Dr. Norman Vincent Peale. His book *A Guide to Confident Living* enabled me to find hope again during a time of deep despair.

It was during a conference for pastors and their spouses that I heard Dr. Peale tell of his own amazing transformation. He said that as a child and teenager he was plagued by feelings of insecurity and inferiority. Then one summer afternoon he took a long walk with his father, a physician and pastor, who got Norman to talk about his fear that he had no ability and would never amount to anything. At one point Norman sat down, first on one tree stump and then on another, while his father described the power of an inferiority complex to ruin a life. He told his son that psychiatric treatment would likely cure him, but that there was no such treatment available in the small town in which they lived.

"However," said his father, "there is a doctor right here who can cure any mental or emotional disease. Norman, are you willing to let this Great Physician, Jesus Christ, heal you?"

Dr. Peale said that the transformation in his life began when he told his father that he was willing to let Christ heal him. He said: "We knelt by one of the stumps, and I surrendered myself and my inferiority feelings to the Great Physician. A strong sense of peace and confidence came over me." He told those of us at the conference that whenever he was tired or overstressed, the feelings would sometimes return, but that he had learned to have victory over them by the power of Christ and the affirmations found in the Bible.

You, too, can overcome feelings of fear, inferiority, and anxiety by internalizing your Christian heritage.

Claim Your God-Given Strength

When we claim our Christian heritage, we can become strong in our spirits as God meant us to be. When I read the Bible, I am struck by the vitality of the people who fill its pages. Abraham and Sarah endured hundreds of miles of travel by camel when they were in their seventies. Then they, who had lived their lives in luxury in Ur of Chaldees, spent their later years in the desert without the benefit of a house. Still, they lived to be 175 and 127 respectively. Moses spent forty years in the wilderness and had unusual stamina even until he was 120 years old (see Deuteronomy 34:7). Miriam, the sister of Moses, not only endured the rigors of the wilderness but also inspired and motivated the children of Israel when they became discouraged. The apostle Paul was a dynamo of a man who endured being shipwrecked, beaten, stoned, and imprisoned. He summarized the secret of his seemingly endless energy in his letter to the Philippians: "I can do all things through Christ who strengthens me" (Philippians 4:13 NKJV). In Matthew 9:20-22, we read the story of the woman who had been hemorrhaging for many years. She was weak physically, but her faith had kept her spirits strong and eventually led to her physical healing.

Certainly Christ was and is a power personality. These were among his last words before ascending into heaven: "All power is given unto me in heaven and in earth" (Matthew 28:18). Then immediately he said, "Go ye therefore. . . ." (v. 19). We have a Savior who expects us to be strong. As we are promised in John 1:12, we are given strength and are physically empowered to fulfill God's purposes in the world. Jesus described this purpose in response to the question asked by the lawyer: "Which is the great commandment?" (Matthew 22:36). He replied: "Thou shalt love the Lord thy God with all thy heart, and with all thy soul, and with all thy mind. This is the first and great commandment. And the second is like unto it, Thou shalt love thy neighbour as thyself" (vv. 37-39). When we claim our God-given strength, we are enabled to realize and use our God-given potential.

Outward Signs of Inward Illness

Today we often think of ourselves as body, mind, and spirit, acting as if we were three entities. Researchers and physicians in the field of psychosomatic medicine have helped us realize that what happens in our minds and spirits affects our bodies, and vice versa. People of faith have known this through the centuries. Two thousand years ago, the apostle Paul wrote: "Beloved, I pray that you may prosper in all things and be in health, just as your soul prospers" (3 John 2 NKJV).

How well I remember conducting a seminar for the employees of a bank. The subject of the seminar was "Stress Without Distress," and we talked about the coping skills we need when our circuits become overloaded. After the seminar, a woman in her early forties stopped to talk with me. She told me how she was suffering from insomnia, stomach pains, and headaches. When I suggested that she see her doctor for a complete physical, she said that she had one only two days before and that all tests were negative. I was sure that something in the mental, emotional, or spiritual area of her life must be responsible for her physical discomfort.

As we talked about her life, I suddenly hit a "raw nerve" when I asked about her family. Venom spewed out of her words as she told me how her sister had received more income from their parents' estate than she had. It was not her parents but her sister whom she blamed. She had not spoken to her sister in the ten years since the will was read. Thinking that she must have been deprived of thousands of dollars, I was stunned to find that the difference was only $120.

Think of it! Ten years she had suffered physical distress and mental torment over the amount of $120. She had spent far more than that in visits to various doctors. Yet, she could see no connection between her resentment and her physical symptoms, and the idea of forgiveness was abhorrent to her. My guess is that she will miss the abundant life that Jesus talked about (see John 10:10) and will go to an early grave from unnecessary illnesses.

Because we are "fearfully and wonderfully made" and are one entity, not three, we need to listen to our bodies. If we have regular colds, stomachaches, headaches, or other recurring health problems, the cause may be something more than a virus or physical disorder. We may be overstressed or angry or resentful or afraid. This can be true even of small children.

When our second son was born, our first-born son, Rick, was only twenty-two months old. From everything we had read, we knew to spend extra time with him as he adjusted to a new brother with whom he was to share his parents' attention. Actually, we felt he was making the adjustment well. He showed no obvious signs of jealousy.

Soon, however, Rick began to awaken each night, crying and saying that his legs hurt. After several trips to the doctor, the wise physician told us that he could find nothing wrong with our son's legs. He suspected that Rick was suffering from the deep fear that his legs couldn't move fast enough to keep him close to us. He was afraid he was losing our love. Upon the doctor's suggestion, we redoubled our efforts and spent even more time holding Rick, reading to him, and reassuring him of our love. It worked like magic. Soon he was sleeping peacefully through the night—and so were we.

A woman in her forties suffers heart palpitations and nausea when she experiences jealousy. She is jealous of her sister's achievements, of her brother's material success, and of any woman who even talks with her husband at a party. She goes to the doctor often for her physical symptoms, but she refuses to acknowledge that the source of her problem may be psychological and spiritual. This kind of experience can happen to any of us. Whether the negative emotion is jealousy, resentment, fear, anger, prejudice, or anxiety, we need to monitor our bodies to see if these emotions accompany physical symptoms of illness or disease.

Many people may not have physical symptoms related to emotional or spiritual sickness, but they lack enthusiasm or zest for living. They are apathetic, negative, lethargic—"the walking dead."

At a wedding reception I was pleased to see two friends I hadn't seen for several years. Though I enjoyed talking with both of them, I was struck with the difference in their energy levels and enthusiasm. The first friend I spoke with was in her sixties, and her life hasn't been a bed of roses. Her husband died about ten years ago, and she had to return to the workforce. This required her to return to school while she reared two teenagers. It wasn't easy, but she persevered. Now she has a good job, and both children are in college. Her conversation was energetic, entertaining, and full of hope for the future.

The other friend was a young woman in her late thirties. She has a good job in the profession of her choice and is married to a successful corporate lawyer. Yet, she was critical of the food being served at the reception, was angry that the mother of the bride had allowed the bride's sister to bring her young children to the reception (their laughter didn't seem to be bothering anyone else), and was skeptical about the future happiness of the bride and groom. Though our conversation lasted only a few minutes, it seemed interminable. There was little substance to what she said and lots of negativism. It was a joy to have another friend walk up and join us.

Later in the evening, I thought of my two encounters. The first was filled with optimism, confidence, and hope and left me feeling enthusiastic and happy. The second was a downer and left me feeling exhausted. No wonder the second woman looked tired and unhappy. Her energy had been drained by negative emotions.

The wholeness that Jesus spoke of when he said, "I have come that [you] may have life, and that [you] may have it more abundantly" (John 10:10 NKJV) is found in walking in daily fellowship with Christ. It is found also in practical ways such as choosing positive emotions, combating stress and anger, improving our interpersonal relationships, and living within our means. We *can* choose to live in power!

Choose to Live in Power

In a fast-paced world where the multitudinous activities and demands can suck the very life out of us, we can choose to live in power. We can claim our Christian heritage and God-given strength, choose positive emotions, and affirm words of promise and encouragement from the Bible, such as:

> The LORD is the strength of my life. (Psalm 27:1)
>
> In quietness and in confidence shall be [my] strength. (Isaiah 30:15)
>
> Be strong and of a good courage, fear not, nor be afraid. (Deuteronomy 31:6)
>
> Be strong and courageous. (2 Chronicles 32:7)
>
> The joy of the LORD is [my] strength. (Nehemiah 8:10)

Though being positive by conditioning our minds with biblical affirmations may not make us physically strong or healthy, it will give us spiritual power. It is spiritual power that enables us to be "up on down days" and to be all that we were created to be.

Steps for Living in Power

1. Remember that you are "fearfully and wonderfully made" (Psalm 139:14).

2. Claim your Christian heritage—created in the image of God, redeemed by Christ, and empowered by the Holy Spirit—and live it. The evidence is a quiet confidence that enables you to release more and more of your potential.

3. Claim your God-given strength by taking care of your body, learning to relax, improving your interpersonal relationships, and walking in daily fellowship with Christ.

4. Remember that you are one entity: body, mind, and spirit. What happens in one area of your life will affect the others.

5. Listen for signals from your body. If you are suffering from fatigue, irritability, headaches, stomachaches, or insomnia, have a physical examination. If no physical cause is indicated, determine whether the symptoms are caused by stress or negative emotions or spiritual negligence. Work out a plan of action and stick to it.

6. Break the habit of negative emotions by breaking the chain of repetition and replacing each negative emotion with confidence, hope, forgiveness, love, or another positive emotion. Remember, the habit of negative emotions is most effectively broken by a daily walk with Christ.

7. Choose to live in power!

9.

LISTEN TO YOUR SELF-TALK

Mary Baldwin was thirty-six when I met her. In social settings she seemed relaxed and positive, but at home—under the pressures of caring for three preschool children and living within a tight budget—Mary reverted to earlier conditioning. She exaggerated the negative, saying things such as, "This is the worst day of my life." She became pessimistic, expecting bad things to happen. Because this was unconscious on her part, she was stunned one day when her husband said, "When I am tired, I dread coming home because of your negativism."

After some angry exchanges, they didn't just hug, make up, and ask each other's forgiveness, though that was the necessary first step. They also worked out a plan of action. Jim agreed to help more with the children, and they planned an evening out each week away from the children. Mary learned to interrupt her negative thoughts with positive self-talk. She would say: "Wait a minute. This isn't the worst day of my life. I can handle this with God's help." She also wore a rubber band on her right wrist. Whenever she began to think negatively, she would pull the band back and let it snap against her wrist. It was an effective reminder to think more positively.

Learn and Practice Faith-Filled Optimism

In the past three decades, research of outstanding psychiatrists, psychologists, and sociologists has helped us understand that optimism and pessimism are primarily learned. In their book *Guide to Rational Living,* psychiatrist Aaron T. Beck and psychologist Albert Ellis challenge long-held views about depression. They argue that depression is not always a result of brain chemistry or anger turned inward; rather, often it is a disorder of conscious thought. In other words, we need to be helped to change our wrong thinking into right thinking!

Perhaps the person who has made this concept most understandable is Martin E. P. Seligman, professor of psychiatry at the University of Pennsylvania. He is the leading authority on "learned helplessness (pessimism)," "learned optimism," and what he calls "explanatory style" or self-talk—what you say to yourself when you experience setbacks. In his book *Learned Optimism,* Seligman suggests that optimism or its opposite, pessimism, is learned basically from our primary caregiver—usually our mother—in the first seven years of life. However, if you have been programmed by pessimistic parents or significant others, you *can* change your programming.

Changing negative programming is important, because optimism is so powerful. Optimism provides bounce-back ability, enabling us to see problems as possibilities, to keep ourselves motivated and energized, and to build up positive esprit de corps in family, job, or other team relationships. Recent studies indicate that optimists excel in their work, have better health, establish long and happy marriages, stay connected to their children, and perhaps even live longer. The studies suggest that this is possible because optimism provides energy and enthusiasm and allows us to be more focused.

In his book *The Power of Optimism,* Dr. Alan Loy

McGinnis suggests that optimists share twelve characteristics. From these characteristics I have developed my own list of twelve important habits of an optimist.

Habits of an Optimist

1. They know that "in the world you will have tribulation" (John 16:33 NKJV), but they see themselves as problem solvers.

2. They chip away at a problem and are not overwhelmed by its enormity.

3. They are confident they can make a difference.

4. They take time to "recharge their batteries"—physically, mentally, and spiritually.

5. They counteract negative thoughts by finding a more positive way of thinking.

6. They look for the kernel of good in bad situations.

7. They visualize victories and happy outcomes.

8. They know the difference between being joyful and being happy, and they are joyful even during difficult times.

9. They consistently set new goals, rather than rest on old laurels.

10. They look for ways to fill their lives with love—through people, causes, ideas, and activities.

11. They don't focus on bad news, and they don't gossip.

12. Since the past can't be changed and many people won't change, optimists dwell on what they *can* change.

It is my own observation that in addition to these habits, optimists endorse the prayer attributed to Reinhold Neibuhr:

> God grant me the serenity to accept the things
> I cannot change,
> The courage to change the things I can,
> And the wisdom to know the difference.

Developing the habits and positive outlook of an optimist may be a "tall order" for some of us. Yet, with God's help, even those of us who tend to have negative dispositions can make some very positive changes. A good place to start is by listening to your self-talk.

Empower Yourself with Positive Self-Talk

One of the most effective ways to become a more positive, optimistic person is through self-talk. Is your self-talk uplifting and affirming, or is it destructive and demeaning? Are you your own worst enemy by constantly saying things like "I'm so dumb! Why do I always do stupid things like that?" or "I'm sure I will fail! I always fail," or "Jan didn't speak to me. Nobody really likes me; I will never have friends!"? Psychologists tell us that our self-talk defines the picture we have of ourselves. The more negative the self-talk, the more we project the picture of an unhappy, incompetent, and defeated person. They suggest that we avoid words such as *always* and *never* because these words personalize everything that happens rather than enable us to look at objective facts. For example, if we make a mistake and want to learn from it, rather than saying, "I'll never accomplish this," we can say, "This is a difficult task, but I have the resources and faith to make it happen; and I will plan carefully."

Golf superstar Arnold Palmer says that when he makes a bad golf shot, he stops immediately and says to himself,

"That wasn't like me. Next time I will do it this way." Then he imagines the way he will do it correctly. When used regularly, affirmations such as this actually condition our minds toward positive belief in ourselves—dispelling fear, apprehension, and disbelief.

The Bible is full of affirmations that enable us to remember that we are not alone. Let these become a natural part of your self-talk. When you face a difficult situation, empower yourself by saying one of these affirmations aloud or silently:

> I can do all things through Christ who strengthens me. (Philippians 4:13 NKJV)
>
> If God be for [me], who can be against [me]? (Romans 8:31)
>
> The secret is simply this: . . . Christ [is] in [us] bringing with him the hope of all the glorious things to come. (Colossians 1:27 J. B. Phillips)
>
> But to all who received him, who believed in his name, he gave power to become children of God. (John 1:12 NRSV)

We are helped to be more optimistic through the joyful knowledge that we are loved and forgiven by God. When we accept this gift of love, made evident to us through the death of Jesus—"For God so loved the world that he gave his only Son, so that everyone who believes in him may not perish but may have eternal life" (John 3:16 NRSV)—we are empowered for living in the here and now.

Jesus Wants You to Live Abundantly

When Jesus states one of his reasons for coming into the world—"I have come that they may have life, and . . . have it more abundantly" (John 10:10 NKJV)—he indicates that we don't have to live as defeated, unhappy human beings. As Paul says in Romans 8:37, "In all these things we are more than conquerors through Him who loved us" (NKJV). The word *abundance* comes from a Latin word that means "to rise up in waves" or "to overflow." Think of God's blessings surging upon us until we say with the psalmist, "My cup runneth over" (Psalm 23:5). This is said a little differently in John 1:16: "And of His fullness we have all received, and grace for grace" (NKJV). Both of these quotations are images of overflowing love—gifts stacked on top of one another.

How do we appropriate this abundance into daily living? We can begin by cultivating the art of awareness. Have you ever gone to the dentist and then spent hours afterward with no feeling in your mouth because it has been numbed by a shot of Novocain? As we walk through life, we sometimes appear to be like people who are filled with Novocain. We do our tasks in robot fashion, seemingly unaware of God's blessings, which are poured out on us in abundance.

One of my favorite dramas is *Our Town* by Thornton Wilder. The story is about Emily Webb, who dies and goes to heaven. Missing her earthly family terribly, she requests permission to return to earth for a brief visit. Permission is granted. She chooses to relive her twelfth birthday. Her one limitation is that no one can see or hear her.

Emily's great discovery is how unaware she had been of the beauty and wonder of life. She sees everyone hurrying to and fro without awareness of the importance of their relationships or the meaning of life. For me, the most poignant words in the entire play are when Emily says, "Mama, Mama, look at me. Look at me just once as if you really saw me." Although we don't have the opportunity to see our lives from an eternal dimension, we can take time and steps to cultivate awareness. One of the first steps is to count our blessings.

Live with Gratitude

In order to appreciate our blessings, perhaps we all need an experience similar to that of a friend of mine.

Her husband traveled most of each week as a sales representative for a pharmaceutical company. Often he asked her to accompany him when his trip was short enough that they could drive. When the children were small, and even when they were teenagers, she had good reason to stay at home because she was needed. But after the children were on their own, she was so in the habit of her routine that she continued to decline his invitations. Then one night she dreamed that during an annual physical examination, the doctor told her that she was terminally ill and had only two months to live. Suddenly she realized how much she loved her husband and how she had wasted so many opportunities when they could have been together. When she awakened, she realized gratefully that it was only a dream and that she still had time to shake herself out of a rut and nurture their relationship.

The words of an old hymn encourage us to see and appreciate the blessings that come to us daily from God's hand:

> Count your many blessings, name them one by one.
> And it will surprise you what the Lord hath done.

As David reminds us in Psalm 92:1, "It is a good thing to give thanks unto the LORD." Giving thanks not only enables us to see and appreciate the abundance of God's blessings, but it also opens our hearts to life, to those around us, and to the very presence of God.

As I've mentioned, I recognized this truth when our oldest son died at age twenty. My grief was overwhelming, hanging over me like a dark cloud. The cloud was there when I went to bed at night and when I awakened each morning. Even my prayers seemed to rise no higher than the ceiling of the room. I was inundated by the heaviness of grief. Then one morning in my quiet time, I read words that I had read before, but this time they seemed to have my name on them—and a message straight from God to me. They were Paul's words to the Thessalonians: "In everything give thanks; for this is the will of God in Christ Jesus for you" (1 Thessalonians 5:18 NKJV). I realized that I wasn't asked to give thanks for the death of our son; rather, in the midst of our tragedy, I was asked to give thanks for all I had left. That very moment I began to thank God for a husband who loved me, for another son of whom we were very proud; for friends who loved and supported us; for a church full of members who surrounded us with their prayers; for a job where I was needed; for faith in God, whose Son also died; and for Jesus, who was intimately acquainted with tragedy during his sojourn here on planet Earth.

Each day as I gave thanks, I could feel the cloud of grief lifting. As I have said, that simple act of thanksgiving so revolutionized my life that I have continued to do it every morning. Before I get out of bed to exercise and have a quiet time, I condition my mind with gratitude. In this way, I "set my sails" for the day. On the rare occasions when I oversleep and fail to do it, I find that I am irritable with others and impatient with myself. The verse I use to "jump-start" my gratitude is Psalm 118:24: "This is the day the LORD has made; [I] will rejoice and be glad in it" (NKJV).

Living with gratitude involves opening your eyes and ears and heart and spirit to experience life as it is happening. It is a reminder to see God's faithfulness. At least once a week, I suggest that you affirm the words of the hymn "Great Is Thy Faithfulness," written by Thomas O. Chisholm:

> Great is thy faithfulness, O God my Father;
> There is no shadow of turning with thee;
> Thou changest not, thy compassions, they fail not;
> As thou hast been, thou forever wilt be.
> Great is thy faithfulness! Great is thy faithfulness!

> Morning by morning new mercies I see;
> All I have needed thy hand hath provided;
> Great is thy faithfulness, Lord, unto me!

As you do this, you will be filled with gratitude for all that God has done and is doing in your life, and you will experience abundant living in its truest sense.

Cultivate Friends

Another way to appropriate the abundance that God has provided is to recognize that we are not meant to live as lonely, alienated human beings. We were created to live in community, in relationship with others. Genesis 2:18 tells us: "It is not good that the man should be alone; I will make him a helper as his partner" (NRSV). More and more I am convinced that far more than creeds or doctrines, the kingdom of God is relationships—our relationship to God through Christ, our relationship to ourselves, and our relationship to others. After all, when Jesus was asked by the lawyer what the greatest commandment was, he said: "Thou shalt love the Lord thy God with all thy heart, and with all thy soul, and with all thy mind. This is the first and great commandment. And the second is like unto it, Thou shalt love thy neighbour as thyself" (Matthew 22:37-39).

Why, then, are so many of us lonely? Dr. Harold Bloomfield, a well-known psychotherapist, said in a television interview that the biggest problem he encounters among his patients today is loneliness. He said that we insulate ourselves in our air-conditioned homes where we sit in front of computers and television sets, becoming less and less relational. What we may not know, however, is that isolating ourselves in this way can be detrimental to our health and well-being. In one of her "Personal

Health" columns for the *New York Times*, Jane Brody wrote that according to the findings of medical researchers, people who have friends they can turn to for encouragement, empathy, advice, help, and affection are more likely to survive health crises such as heart attacks and major surgery. What's more, they are less likely to develop diseases such as cancer and respiratory infections. In addition to the physical advantages of friendship, all of us can attest to the mental, emotional, and spiritual "boosts" we often experience when we are with friends. Friends can "recharge our batteries" and expand our horizons. Friends not only make us feel better; they actually make us better friends ourselves.

Think of a person you know who is well liked by others. What are this person's characteristics? My guess is that he or she is genuinely friendly. The book of Proverbs tells us that one who has friends "must himself [or herself] be friendly" (18:24 NKJV). Persons who have many friends are usually interested in other people. They are kind and encouraging. They also are interesting conversationalists, because they have learned to care for other people and have the ability to draw others out of themselves. They always can be counted on to "be there" for a friend, no matter what the circumstances may be. They know the true value of a friend.

In our increasingly technological and impersonal world, it is so important to cultivate friends—particularly a few close Christian friends who can provide support and encouragement for our Christian walk through this world. In addition to building one another up (see Romans 15:2) and bearing one another's burdens (see Galatians 6:2), Christian friends can help us remember our Christian heritage and remain strong in our faith—even in the most difficult of times.

One of my favorite New Testament characters is Barnabas, who lived up to the meaning of his name: "son of encouragement." It was Barnabas who was there for Paul, encouraging the apostles—who were still wary of Paul because he had persecuted the Christians—to accept him. When Paul retreated to Tarsus, it was Barnabas who brought him back into the church (see Acts 11:25-26). And later when Paul refused to take young John Mark on his second missionary journey, it was Barnabas who stood by John Mark, encouraging him back into the Lord's work (see Acts 15:36-39). Barnabas is a good model of Christian friendship.

Remember That God Loves You Personally

Proverbs 18:24 tells us about the Ultimate Friend who "sticketh closer than a brother." That friend, of course, is God made evident to us through Jesus Christ. "God is love" (1 John 4:8), and his love for us is seen throughout the Bible. I like to think of the entire Bible as a compilation of love letters from God to us. When I feel down or lonely, I affirm some of his many love notes. I have found that the best kind of self-talk is repeating Scripture verses. These are among my favorites:

> I have loved thee with an everlasting love: therefore with lovingkindness have I drawn thee. (Jeremiah 31:3)
> For God so loved [substitute your name], that he gave his only begotten Son. (John 3:16)
> We love him, because he first loved us. (1 John 4:19)
> Who shall separate us from the love of Christ? (Romans 8:35)
> The God of love and peace shall be with you. (2 Corinthians 13:11)

You may wonder how God can love you *individually*, since there are so many people in the world. I used to wonder that until one day I thought about my grandmother, who had eleven children yet had plenty of love for each of them. Every one of those children seemed to be special to Grandmother Feree. Then I recalled Susanna Wesley, wife of a nineteenth-century Anglican clergyman, Samuel Wesley. When I feel overwhelmed by my responsibilities as wife, mother, grandmother, and friend, I think of Susanna. In addition to her responsibilities as a minister's wife and homemaker, she home-schooled her nineteen children. She also spent an hour with each of them for spiritual training each week. Two of her children, John and Charles, became great spiritual leaders who founded the Methodist movement, and according to a prominent English historian, saved England from a fate similar to the French Revolution. If Susanna Wesley, an intelligent but normal human being, could love each of her nineteen children, how much more does an infinite God love each of us?

We need to live joyfully in the knowledge of God's love. Positive self-talk, particularly when it includes biblical affirmations, "stir[s] up the gift of God" (2 Timothy 1:6) within us. It energizes us, gives us hope, and causes us to remember that "the joy of the LORD is your strength" (Nehemiah 8:10).

Steps for Living Abundantly

1. Learn and practice faith-filled optimism. Optimism and pessimism are largely learned thought patterns. You *can* change wrong thinking into right thinking!

2. Listen to your self-talk. Keep a record periodically to determine the picture you have of yourself.

3. Replace negative self-talk and empower yourself with biblical affirmations.

4. Believe with confidence that you can make a difference. According to Dr. Alan Loy McGinnis, author of *The Power of Optimism,* this belief is one of the common habits shared by optimists.

5. Remember that Jesus wants you to live abundantly. In John 10:10, Jesus says: "I have come that [you] may have life, and that [you] may have it more abundantly" (NKJV).

6. Appropriate this abundance into your everyday living through a heightened awareness of God's blessings.

7. Practice and live each day with gratitude, because gratitude opens your heart to life, to those around you, and to the very presence of God.

8. Cultivate abundance by making and nurturing friendships. The blueprint for this was given in Jesus' emphasis on the two great commandments (see Matthew 22:37-39).

9. Remember that God loves you personally, and that Jesus is the Ultimate Friend.

10.

LISTEN TO YOUR DREAMS

I have no memory of what he looked like, and I don't even remember his name, but the commencement speaker at my high school graduation said two sentences that have been seared into my brain: "The world is not looking for people who make excuses but for people who do something. That always starts with a dream."

My dream was to go to college. However, because my father was going through some serious financial difficulties at the time, it was assumed that I would go to work as soon as I graduated from high school. My dream had been laid aside, or at least put on the back burner. The commencement speaker stirred the fires of my imagination and allowed me to dream again.

Though I did go to work the day after graduation and said nothing to my parents about my dream, I never went to bed at night or awakened in the morning without seeing myself graduating from the college of my choice. On Sunday following the commencement address, the minister in our church preached on Matthew 17:20: "If you have faith the size of a mustard seed, you will say to this mountain, 'Move from here to there,' and it will move" (NRSV).

My mountain didn't move immediately, but later that summer my family moved to a neighboring town. I became very active in the youth program of our new church. My best friend, Margaret, was the minister's daughter. She was vivacious, fun-loving, and college-bound. My dream became stronger, and by the time she left for college, I knew that I, too, would go, though I didn't know how or when.

During that year, as I worked to earn money, our minister investigated scholarships for me. If my faith ever began to waver, he would remind me of two Bible verses that became the foundation stones for my dream: "But with God all things are possible" (Matthew 19:26), and "I can do all things through Christ who strengthens me" (Philippians 4:13 NKJV).

My faith in Christ was growing faster and stronger than my dream. As I became active in a Bible study, I began to see how God reveals his will for our lives. In addition, I began to grow in leadership skills, especially with young people and Sunday school teachers. The pieces were beginning to fit together. I could see why God wanted me to go to college—not only to be educated, but also to serve him. It was an exciting realization—one that motivated me to keep on believing in my dream.

The Power of Believing

Even now, I am amazed at how God provides people and circumstances to enable us to fulfill our God-given dreams. How do we know if they are God's dreams? How do we distinguish between wishful thinking, personal desires, and God-given dreams? My own experience is that the latter keeps resurfacing in my mind with growing intensity. Ask yourself this question: "If this became a reality, would it hurt me or anyone else? Is there anything in the dream that is not in keeping with God's will as exemplified by Christ?"

When a dream seems to be in sync with God's will, then hold fast to the dream, stay firmly rooted in the Christian faith, work toward the realization of the dream, never give up, and watch doors begin to open. Before I set foot on the campus of my choice, I had enough scholarship and work opportunities to take me through four years of undergraduate studies. Those were four of the happiest years of my life. My dream had been realized; I experienced the exciting power of believing!

Translate Your Dreams into Action

Some people say that they have dreams when what they actually have are wishes. A wish becomes a dream when it is combined with expectation and conviction. A dream is translated into action when it has a definite purpose. French essayist Michel de Montaigne wrote, "No wind favors him who has no destined port."

Determine Your Purpose

Thoughts are living things because they empower our attitudes, our actions, and our habits. One of the most important thoughts we will ever hold is *my life matters*. This thought will lead us to make a positive contribution to the world in which we live. Edward F. Kennedy was a man who lived with purpose. He once said: "Few will have the greatness to bend history itself, but each of us can work to change a small portion of events. . . . It is from numberless acts of courage and belief that human history is shaped." If we choose not to live purposefully, we abandon our gifts and talents and destroy the creative force within us. Often what results is apathy, disease, drug use, alcohol abuse, and suicide.

David McNally, author and president of Trans-Form Corporation, told about the following experience in an article he wrote on "The Power of Purpose." He said that on a business trip he had his shoes professionally shined for the first time. The man who shined them was a master craftsman named Zee. Zee treated his shoes as if they were the finest pair he had ever shined. Zee's enthusiasm was so infectious that he was rewarded by a long line of people waiting for his services. When asked about his business, he said that he was happy and loved what he was doing. McNally wrote: "I learned that what you do is not as important as how or why you do it. Zee had used the principle of contribution to create a modest but successful business. He had much to teach larger and more sophisticated companies who had lost sight of their primary purpose."

Set Specific Goals

After determining your purpose—your primary purpose in life and your purpose for a specific endeavor—it is necessary to set specific goals. After much soul-searching, I determined that my primary purpose in life is to know Christ and to make him known. At that time in my life, it seemed that I could do this best through full-time service in the church as a director of Christian education. The specific goals I set were to go to college, to learn as much as possible about my profession, to learn people skills, to walk in daily fellowship with Christ, and to find a position in a church. My dream remained in the dream stage until I had a specific purpose with specific goals—until I knew *why* I wanted to go to college, *where* I wanted to go, and *when* I could expect to get there. Then, and only then, could I translate my dream into action.

Practice the Power of Faith

In addition to purpose and goals, a dream requires the power of faith. Dr. Daniel Poling's son was one of the four interfaith chaplains who helped people into lifeboats as their ship went down during World War II. The chaplains, with their arms locked and their heads bowed in prayer, went down in the South Pacific with their ship. For months after the death of his son, Dr. Poling would say to himself: "I believe. I believe. I believe." He said that he would do this early each morning to drive doubt and discouragement from his mind. Then he would add: "In all these things we are more than conquerors through Him who loved us" (Romans 8:37 NKJV). It was the power of faith that helped him to escape the pit of despair.

We cultivate faith in many ways—through daily Bible reading, prayer, and meditation as well as by participating in Sunday school, study groups, and corporate worship. Regularly practicing these habits keeps us in tune with God's will and purposes. Often it is in times of silence and worship that we are most receptive to a dream from God. My own experience has been that God's dream often seems too big for us when the idea first comes. It requires stretching to learn new skills and to use previously ignored gifts. But God doesn't give impossible dreams. We must never give up on a dream because it seems too big. Instead we should take that first step to learn a new skill and develop our gifts. It is amazing how the doors will open before us. God's dreams call us into the future.

Cultivate the "E-Factor"

Another element necessary for translating dreams into action is the "E-Factor." Perhaps no one I know embodies the "E-Factor" more than Joe Dresnok. I had heard of his leadership and relational skills, particularly his ability to motivate others, from employees of his business consulting company, but my first encounter with him exceeded all I had heard. He literally exuded energy, enthusiasm, and vitality. I was impressed by his aliveness. In fact, meeting and talking with him made me feel as if I had just received a B-12 shot!

The "E-Factor" is not included in the usual list of job skills sought in an employee—things such as knowledge of economics, accounting, marketing, or computer skills—yet its importance is being stressed more and more by businesses today. The "E-Factor" is an invisible factor, the results of which are clearly evident. Basically, it is sustained enthusiasm.

What is enthusiasm? The famous English historian Arnold Toynbee wrote that apathy is overcome only by enthusiasm. Enthusiasm, he said, is aroused by two things: an ideal that takes the imagination by storm, and a definite, intelligible plan for putting that ideal into practice. Most observers agree that enthusiasm is a dynamic quality that brings the personality alive, releasing dormant powers. It includes personal initiative, self-discipline, and perseverance. Those who possess it are self-motivated, energetic individuals who work well with others and create a climate of excitement and expectation. Although it is generally seen in those who are outgoing, it also can be found in the quiet strength of a more private person. In either case, it is not backslapping, phony exuberance or loud laughter.

Most people who have studied enthusiasm agree on two things: It is a skill that can be acquired, and it makes a vast difference in one's life. Ralph Waldo Emerson wrote: "Nothing great was ever achieved without enthusiasm." Actually, the word *enthusiasm* comes from two Greek words: "in theos," meaning "God within." I'm convinced that when we truly believe in God and seek to live in his purposes, we are empowered to do more than we believe possible. In Mark 9:23 we read: "All things are possible to him that believeth."

So how do we acquire the skill of enthusiasm? In his booklet on enthusiasm, Dr. Norman Vincent Peale suggests some practical helps for becoming more enthusiastic. Among them are:

Stay sensitized to the thrill of living.

Hold the image of an enthusiastic you in your consciousness.

Act as if you have enthusiasm.

Start each day with enthusiastic thoughts.

Put vitality-activating quotations and Bible passages into your mind to spur enthusiasm.

Love life and people.

These practical suggestions are effective in business as well as in personal life. I once heard a successful business owner say that if he were trying to choose between two prospective employees with fairly equal ability, he would choose the enthusiastic one because that person could motivate himself or herself and others.

Perhaps most important of all, enthusiasm keeps us strong for living. Once while reading about a brass foundry, I saw a wonderful analogy between the molten brass and people. When the brass is heated in a crucible to a temperature of 2,200 degrees Fahrenheit, it becomes very strong. In fact, it cannot be broken. On the other hand, when it is allowed to cool, it becomes very brittle. Likewise, when we are surcharged with spiritual fire and enthusiasm, nothing can break us. But if we let the spiritual fire and enthusiasm die down, even the small blows of circumstance can crack and shatter us. If we want to stay strong, we have to keep the "E-Factor" operative!

Slay Your Giants

If your dream comes true, it won't be without courage to overcome obstacles in your path. At times you may feel like David fighting the giant, Goliath. Read again this inspiring story found in 1 Samuel 17.

David was a teenager, too young to join his older brothers who were fighting in the Israelite army against the Philistines. He was a shepherd boy. That must have been a lonely task, far from the excitement and dangers of battle—though David did have encounters from time to time with wild animals that attacked the sheep. Still, he must have been thrilled when his father asked him to deliver a "care package" of bread, parched corn, and cheese to his brothers on the battlefront. When he arrived, he couldn't believe his eyes. There was a huge giant of a man parading on a hilltop and challenging any Hebrew to a duel.

"Choose a man to fight me," the giant yelled. "If he kills me, we Philistines will be your slaves; but if I win, you Hebrews will become our slaves" (1 Samuel 17:8-9, author's paraphrase).

David couldn't believe that no one volunteered to fight. After all, the Philistines were the Israelite's worst enemies. They worshiped pagan gods and had lewd sexual practices including temple prostitution. David asked, "Who is this uncircumcised Philistine that he should defy the armies of the living God?" (1 Samuel 17:26 NRSV).

Since no one had agreed to a duel with Goliath, David volunteered to fight the giant, despite his brother's efforts to dissuade him. King Saul was delighted to have a volunteer, and he offered his armor to David. Of course, it was much too large, so David took his own equipment—a slingshot and five smooth stones—and went to fight with the power of God.

When Goliath saw a young, seemingly unarmed boy coming to fight him, he roared with laughter. "Come to me," he shouted, "and I will give your flesh to the birds of the air and to the wild animals of the field" (1 Samuel 17:44 NRSV).

Walking confidently toward the giant, the young teenager shouted back, "You come to me with a sword and a spear and a shield, but I come to you in the name of the LORD of Hosts. This day the LORD will deliver you into my hand and I will take off your head. It is the carcasses of the Philistines that will be food for the birds and beasts" (1 Samuel 17:45-46, author's paraphrase). That was good psychological warfare! We remember the end of the story. David killed the giant, and the Philistine army was routed. The Israelite nation rejoiced.

When fulfilling any worthy dream, there are giants to slay—giants such as rejection, ridicule, worry, lack of finances—but none are more destructive than discouragement and fear.

The Giant of Discouragement

Persistence is the weapon necessary to slay the giant of discouragement, or the temptation to give up. When I think of the value of persistence, I think of DeWitt Wallace. In 1921, when Westinghouse downsized because of a recession, Wallace lost his job. He decided to pursue an idea he had long held: to publish a reader's service containing articles of value that were condensed to save time and issued in a small, pocket-sized magazine. He approached some of the well-known publishers of his time, and they all turned him down. But DeWitt Wallace and his wife, Lila, believed in his idea, and in 1922 they started putting out their little magazine themselves. When they died, the magazine had thirty million subscribers and one hundred million readers worldwide. The magazine is the *Reader's Digest*, and it is perhaps the greatest publishing story of all time. DeWitt Wallace was persistent; he slayed the giant of discouragement.

Two scripture verses remind us that no matter what the obstacles, with God's help, *we can overcome.*

> We are afflicted in every way,
> but not crushed; perplexed,
> but not driven to despair;
> persecuted, but not
> forsaken; struck down, but
> not destroyed.
> (2 Corinthians 4:8-9 NRSV)

The Giant of Fear

Of all the giants we may face in the pursuit of our God-given dreams, fear may be the most debilitating. It paralyzes us and keeps us from taking the steps necessary for success. Ralph Waldo Emerson tells us to "do the thing you fear and the death of fear is certain."

Carolyn McNeil was probably the most creative girl in my college class. She played the piano with such skill that her professors encouraged her to become a concert pianist. Yet, except when she was required to do so, Carolyn would not give a concert or even play publicly because she was afraid of failure. She practiced for hours each day in the music building and was better than any of the other students, but she never felt that she was ready to perform. She was paralyzed by fear.

Carolyn also was a talented artist. Her watercolor and oil paintings were the talk of the campus. She received numerous invitations to have a showing of her work or to participate in a regional art exhibit, and she truly wanted to accept. Each time we would think she was going to participate, but at the last minute she would be inundated by fear and remain unable to take the necessary step.

Carolyn was a "ten talent" girl who easily could have been a professional in music or art. Unfortunately, she allowed fear to banish her to the sidelines of life. When I saw her several years ago, she was still playing the piano and painting a bit at home, but she never used her talents to serve others or to glorify God. The giant of fear had won!

The Creator invites us to dream his dream and keep on dreaming as long as we live. Dreams energize us, provide purpose for living, and give us hope. We catch God's dream when we spend time with him—in Bible reading, creative thinking, prayer, and worship. The dream becomes a reality as we understand the purpose of the dream, set specific goals, and take action with enthusiasm and persistence, never giving up.

Steps for Listening to Your Dreams

1. Listen to your heartfelt, deep-seated dreams. "Prayer is the soul's sincere desire, unuttered or expressed."

2. Distinguish between wishes and dreams. A wish is a thought that passes quickly through your mind. You may have many wishes in a day, such as, "I wish I had more time, more money, more energy, fewer pounds . . ." and so forth. A dream will resurface in your mind with ever-increasing intensity and desire. A wish becomes a dream when combined with expectation, conviction, purpose, goals, hard work, faith, and enthusiasm.

3. Be sure your dream is God's dream. Ask yourself: "Is there anything in this dream that will hurt me or anyone else? Is there anything that is not in keeping with God's purpose revealed through Jesus Christ? Will others be blessed by the dream?"

4. Memorize these "foundation stones" for a God-given dream: Matthew 19:26 and Philippians 4:13. Recite them whenever you feel yourself losing the dream or growing discouraged.

5. Remember that the enthusiasm factor is vital for the realization of dreams, and cultivate it daily. Even if you do not feel enthusiastic, try to "act as if" you do.

6. Expect obstacles, and be prepared to overcome them.

7. Arm yourself to slay the giants of discouragement and fear by keeping your faith strong, doing the thing you fear, trusting God's promises, and knowing that "with God all things are possible" (Matthew 19:26).

8. Always remember that a creative God invites you to keep on dreaming.

IV.

Act

11.

Be Decisive

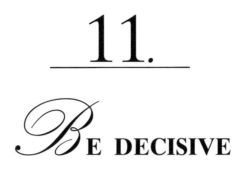

Recently I stopped by a mall to pick up a few items. Because it was almost lunchtime and my husband was out of town, I decided to have a quick lunch at the cafeteria. Directly in front of me was a woman, appearing to be in her mid to late forties, who was indecisive about every item. At first, it was amusing to watch. She took a long time to decide which salad to choose, but even after choosing, she said to herself, "No. I had tossed salad last night. I think I will get carrot and raisin salad." The person behind the counter graciously exchanged the salads. Then the woman looked carefully at the carrot salad and remembered that she had carrots in her tossed salad last night, so she exchanged it for fruit.

She exhibited the same indecision at each counter. By the time we got to the entrees, the people in line behind her were calling out, "Who's holding up the line?" and walking past her with their trays in hand. It was sad to see a woman of her age caught so tightly in the web of indecision.

Life is meant to be lived, not just talked about. Jesus said: "Not everyone who says to me, 'Lord, Lord,' will enter the kingdom of heaven, but only the one who does the will of my Father in heaven" (Matthew 7:21 NRSV). Likewise, in Philippians 4:13, Paul didn't say, "I can *think* all things," or "I can *say* all things," but "I can *do* all things through Christ who strengthens me" (NKJV, emphasis added).

Are You Anchored by Central Certainties?

Being decisive doesn't mean that we have to act impetuously or thoughtlessly or without guidance. It does mean that we have our lives anchored in what I call central certainties, which are guiding truths or principles found in God's Word. Some of these central certainties are:

> God is love. (1 John 4:8)
>
> For God so loved the world, that he gave his only begotten Son, that whosoever believeth in him should not perish, but have everlasting life. (John 3:16)
>
> I [Christ] am the way, and the truth, and the life. No one comes to the Father except through me. (John 14:6 NRSV)
>
> I will pray the Father, and he shall give you another Comforter, that he may abide with you for ever. (John 14:16)
>
> Thou shalt love the Lord thy God with all thy heart, and with all thy soul, and with all thy mind. This is the first and great commandment. And the second is like unto it, Thou shalt love thy neighbour as thyself. (Matthew 22:37-39)

These and other central certainties tell us 90 percent of what we need to know about how to live. With our belief system intact, we are to see ourselves as persons of worth—not because of what we have achieved, but because of what God through Christ has done for us. From there we are to show compassion, to love our neighbors and serve them in the name of Christ. We are to share our faith and live in close fellowship with Christ, so that our personalities reflect love, joy, peace, patience, kindness, generosity, faithfulness, gentleness, and self-control (see Galatians 5:22-23). For the remaining 10 percent of life's questions that we must wrestle with, God gives us good minds and divine guidance. That's a great deal! Why don't we take him up on it?

Recently I saw a "Peanuts" cartoon in which Charlie Brown asked Linus what he wanted to be when he grew up. Linus replied, "I'm going to be a fanatic." "What kind of fanatic?" asked Charlie Brown. Linus thought for a minute and said, "I think I will be a wishy-washy one." We laugh at that because being a wishy-washy fanatic is a contradiction in terms.

Jesus modeled the alternative. He was balanced and whole—never fanatical and never wishy-washy. He was anchored at the core of his being by central certainties, and these allowed him to stretch, to be flexible, and to grow.

I don't know what caused the woman in the cafeteria to be indecisive. My guess is that she had some emotional hang-up. But I do know what caused my own indecision about jumping into deep water after weeks of swimming lessons. It was terrifying fear—fear of not being in control and of drowning.

It was 1957. I was the only female in our family—with one husband, two sons, and even a male dog. I had to do all kinds of "masculine things." They liked to fish, hike, camp, water-ski, and most of all, swim. Now I could swim in shallow water, but I was terrified of deep water.

When our youngest son advanced from swimming in the shallow end to swimming in the deep end of the pool, I took my pride in hand and joined an adult beginner's class. I got along well in the class until the day when the instructor said, "Today we are going to the deep end of the pool." I was very "Christian"—I let everybody go ahead of me! Standing at the other end of the pool, she said to each member of the class, one at a time, "Jump in." Finally, only she and I were standing outside the pool, and she said, "Jump in." I looked down at the deep water and everything in me rebelled. I said, "I can't. I just can't do it." Then she asked me this question: "Do you believe that this water will hold you up?" I could see that it was holding up all the others, and I knew it was the same water that had been holding me up in the shallow end. So I said, "Yes, I believe it will." She replied, "If you believe it, act like you do. Jump in."

I closed my eyes, thought of the good life I had had, and jumped in—never really expecting to come out of that water. I learned what the others in the class already knew: It was easier to swim in deep water.

Later, as I thought about the incident, I realized that there is a spiritual analogy here. As Christians, we say that we believe in God the Father; in Jesus his Son, our Savior; in the Holy Spirit; in the Bible; and in the church as the Body of Christ. Well, if we do, let's act as if we do! We must turn loose of indecision and fear, trust God, and jump into life with faith, hope, and love.

Are You Plugged into the Power Source?

It's not easy to "jump in" with decisiveness when we are feeling down. Often when I feel down, it is the result of not staying plugged into the Power Source. At times I allow the pressures and hassles of daily living to pile up. One extra thing to do or one more trying situation can send me crashing downward. At these times I am trying to do everything by my own strength, and the result is that my spiritual batteries are no longer charged. I know what needs to be done. I need to "be still, and know that [he is] God" (Psalm 46:10); to allow my parched spirit to be refreshed by the living water. Yet I have neither the will nor the motivation to do it.

Once I read the story of a farmer who was plowing in his field on a hot August day. He looked up and saw a handsome young man dressed in a white suit striding across the field toward him. Curious and also glad for a moment of rest, he waited for the man to approach. The young man, a salesman for a new book on farming, asked the farmer, "Would you like your farm to be more productive?" "Yep," said the farmer. "Then if you will follow the author's instructions in this book, you will double your production in two years—guaranteed." The young man described how many copies of the book had been sold and what the amazing results had been.

After a flawless sales pitch, the salesman turned to the farmer and asked, "Well, will you buy one?" "Nope," the farmer said as he leaned against the plow. "Why not?" asked the young man in surprise. "I already know more about what to do than I am doing," replied the farmer.

Isn't that our situation? At those times when life has overwhelmed us, we have forgotten that Jesus said: "I am the vine, you are the branches. Those who abide in me and I in them bear much fruit, because apart from me you can do nothing" (John 15:5 NRSV). When our deeds don't square with our words, it's often because we haven't been plugged into the Power Source.

Are You Part of the Problem or the Solution?

Perhaps a good test for our actions as Christians is whether we are a part of the problem or the solution. We can't pick up a newspaper or listen to radio or television without hearing about problems—problems in our community, our state, our nation, our world. Add those to our personal problems and we often feel powerless, like a drowning person going down for the third time. The great temptation is to make ourselves comfortable in our little corner of the world and feel that we never can make a difference in the world.

There are times when I wish that God had created the world and all its creatures, and then programmed us to live together in peace. But that is only when I feel discouraged. When I am thinking rationally, I give thanks for the wonderful gift of free will—our freedom to choose. I'm grateful, too, that God didn't "finish" the world but has allowed us to have a hand in its completion. This way we have new discoveries to make, new challenges to reach, new solutions to find. What an exciting opportunity! I sometimes wonder what marvelous things will be discovered in the next fifty years. It's easy to understand what the editor who was about to be beheaded in the French Revolution meant when he said, "It's too bad to take off my head. I wanted to see how it all was coming out." For better or worse, we are not like spectators watching an athletic event. We are players in the thick of the game. The question is, are we part of the problem or the solution?

Once I saw a television interview with a renowned plastic surgeon. His mission in life is to help children smile. When a child has a facial disfiguration, his surgery gives the child reason to smile and a sense of self-worth. Not only does he do this for children who come to his clinic, but he also takes a team of plastic surgeons to Third World countries where they serve without remuneration. He said, "I believe that instead of complaining about problems we can't do anything about, we should do something about the ones we can."

When I heard the surgeon speak, I thought of my friend Julie Ragland, a young woman from Chattanooga, Tennessee, who is making a difference in northwest Pasadena, California—formerly one of the worst crime areas in Pasadena. Julie, a vivacious, fun-loving girl, had many advantages when she was growing up: lots of friends; a loving, Christian family; a strong church background; and an excellent education. As a college student,

Julie's strong Christian faith motivated her to work with inner-city children. During her junior year, she was invited to visit a friend who was a student at Fuller Seminary in Pasadena. At the time, her friend was volunteering at Harambee Center, a Christian neighborhood center begun by Mr. and Mrs. John Perkins for the children of that area. Having read of the Perkinses' previous work in Mississippi, Julie admired their strong Christian convictions and the results they had achieved in breaking the cycle of welfare, poverty, and dependency by teaching moral values, skills, self-worth, and faith. She was thrilled to meet them. After returning to Tennessee for her senior year at the university, Julie found that the Perkinses' positive and compelling dream was often on her mind. After graduation, she went to work as a summer volunteer at Harambee Center and soon became a full-time staff member.

While in Los Angeles one summer, my husband and I drove up to visit Julie at the center. We were amazed at what we saw. All the children were clean, well groomed, polite, courteous, well mannered, and articulate. The quality of academic achievement was impressive. We heard a class of first graders reciting poetry that most students don't learn until high school. Not long after our visit, Julie became assistant principal of a newly organized school modeled after the academically superior schools for inner-city children begun in Chicago by Marva Collins. One of the goals for such schools is to have high expectations of the students while surrounding them with love and affection.

Recently, Julie returned to Chattanooga for a visit and spoke to my Sunday school class about her work. She spoke with the excitement of one who has found her God-given dream. There is no doubt about it: This beautiful young woman is a part of the solution. She is making a difference for good and for God.

Each of us can make a difference in this world; in fact, that is precisely what God calls us to do. We don't have to do something dramatic in order to be part of the solution, because even the simplest of actions can make a dramatic difference in someone's life. That's where it all begins: One person helping another. And when we help others, we also help ourselves. Serving others in the name of Christ is one of the best ways to move beyond our own worries and concerns and find true joy. It's a guaranteed remedy for down days.

Steps for Making a Difference

1. Learn to be decisive, focused, purposeful. Start with simple steps, such as giving yourself a deadline for making a decision. For example, if you are planning to paint your bedroom, write down a date when the decision needs to be made. Then write a list of things that need to be done or considered before you make the final decision. This list might include talking with an interior designer at a paint store and bringing home samples of paint colors. Make a decision by the appointed time, and don't waffle. Even if you make a mistake, it isn't the end of the world; it's much better than living in indecision. This process won't be easy the first time you do it, but you will gain confidence and a sense of freedom as you become more decisive.

2. Anchor yourself with central certainties from God's Word. One of the certainties is that God loves and forgives us. When we accept this gift, we become "new creations," exhibiting the fruit of the Spirit (see 2 Corinthians 5:17; Galatians 5:22-23). When we stay connected to Christ, we are creative, joyful, energized, and productive — able to love and serve God and others (see John 15:1-5).

3. Recognize that lack of motivation often comes from lethargy and fear. We overcome lethargy by becoming more decisive, purposeful, and organized. We overcome fear by increasing our faith and by courageously doing the thing we fear.

4. Remember that you are not a spectator in the game of life. You are a player in the thick of the game.

5. Resolve to be part of the solution for life's problems, not part of the problem. One of the best ways to do this is to write down a problem about which you are concerned. Think and pray about it during your quiet time. Then write down one action, however small, that you can take to make a positive difference. Then do it! You will relieve your frustration and hopelessness, and you will be part of the solution.

12.

ACT WITH JOY

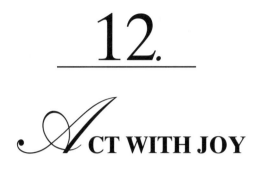

Knowing that he is in excruciating pain every day because of injuries sustained in a mountain climbing accident, I asked Tim Hansel, "How can you be so joyful?" The tall, articulate, joyful man who was speaking in our church replied,"Every day I choose joy. You can choose to be joyous, or you can choose to be miserable. The choice is yours." Immediately a sentence from Barbara Johnson's book *Splashes of Joy in the Cesspools of Life* flashed into my mind: "Pain is inevitable, but misery is optional."

"But if you think I'm joyful," continued Tim, "you should know my friend Mark Spickman. He's a college football coach who has no hands. He uses hooks and has become quite adept at it. In fact, in addition to coaching football, he rides a bike, plays tennis, and lives a very normal life."

Tim told me about going grocery shopping with Mark when he had left his hooks at home. Whenever Mark wanted an item from the shelf, he caught it between his two wrists and dropped it into the grocery cart. As he was reaching up to get a box of cereal, Mark saw two little boys watching in wide-eyed amazement. He was ready for their question: "Mister, what happened to your hands?"

In mock surprise, Mark looked down and said, "Oh my goodness, where are they? I must have left them up in the cereal." Immediately the little boys started looking through the cereal boxes to find the hands.

Then Mark said, "Oh, I remember!"

"What?" chorused the boys.

"Well, when I showered this morning, I left my hands lying on the lavatory."

Isn't that wonderful? In the midst of a difficult situation, Mark Spickman chose to react with joy.

Misconceptions About Joy

There are many things joy is not. Some people think that joy is an attribute dependent upon good health, but I know many healthy individuals who are physically fit yet gloomy, critical, and negative. On the other hand, I have a friend whose spirit is held hostage in a body wracked by the pain of recurring malignancies; and when I am around her, my spirit soars. She is full of laughter and joy.

Some people think that joy is derived from material possessions. Granted, it seems incredible that people who live in the cycle of poverty, spending every waking moment trying to secure the barest necessities, could ever be joyful. Yet one of my most vivid memories is of working in Poland after World War II. Those people had lost everything. Despite the fact that their homes had been destroyed, their country was in rubble from repeated bombings, and almost everyone had lost a loved one in the holocaust or the war, they were a delightful people, full of joy and hope.

Some people believe that joy is the direct result of circumstances. They say such things as: "I could be joyful, too, if my daughter had not become rebellious"; "If I didn't have to endure an unwanted divorce after twenty-four years of marriage, I could be full of joy"; "If I hadn't lost my job in my company's merger, I could be happy."

Most of us have heard similar expressions on many occasions. Life is difficult! From my own experience, I know that you can't walk away from the grave of your twenty-year-old son without tears or a heavy heart, but I also know that in the midst of tragedy, something can sing inside us.

The root word for happiness is *happenstance;* accordingly, happiness is often dependent upon circumstances. A promotion, a wedding, a new baby, a new car, a new house—all of these give us a feeling of pleasure and happiness. But *joy* is a far deeper emotion.

Some people believe that joy is dependent upon your temperament. The Greeks held the theory that each person is born with a certain cast of personality that remains practically unmodified throughout life. The four chief personality types, they said, are sanguine, phlegmatic, choleric, and melancholic. The determinists say that we are one of these types and that we can't do anything about it. They believe that joyful people belong to the first group. People with a sanguine personality are born with bright, sunny, and joyful personalities. If you are in one of the other groups—well, tough luck. You are destined to be unemotional, hot-tempered, or inclined to misery until you die. Obviously, all of us have genetic traits that combine to give us our basic temperament, but we don't have to be a prisoner of our own inheritance. We can make changes—even dramatic changes—by the help of God. Millions of people have been set free. The phlegmatic sparkle, the choleric are urbane, and the melancholic bubble with joy. There is a power that is greater than temperament. It is the power of God through Christ living within us.

Joy Is a Gift from God

Joy is not a human achievement; it is a gift from God. On Broadway, Mary Martin used to sing: "A song is not a song until you sing it; love is not love until you give it away." I'd like to add, "A gift is not a gift until you receive it."

The gift of joy is the miracle of a life in whom Christ lives. This miracle was so visible in the life of the apostle Paul. This myriad-minded man had many important things to say in his thirteen letters found in the New Testament, but one thing he said over and over again was this: "in Christ." The eminent German scholar Adolph Deissman counted the number of times Paul used this phrase, or sister phrases such as "in him" or "in the Lord," and found that it came to 164. It was the key to all that Paul had to say. The joyful life, the victorious life, is found by letting Christ live in us.

Some people have said that because Paul was a moral genius and so deeply spiritual, he never should be used as a model for ordinary men and women. No doubt he was a genius and a mystic; yet when he spoke of being "in Christ," he did not mean some visionary or mystical experience but a necessary experience for the abundant life of which Jesus spoke: "I have come that they may have life, and that they may have it more abundantly" (John 10:10 NKJV). For me, the meaning of being "in Christ" is a simple, daily surrender of my will to Christ. Paul spoke of this when he said, "I die daily" (1 Corinthians 15:31). It is simple but not easy, because our lives are so ego-centered. A good way to begin is to ask daily, "What are *we* going to do today?" rather than "What am *I* going to do today?"

Paul's expressions of the experience of being in Christ are found throughout his letters. For example, "If anyone is in Christ, there is a new creation" (2 Corinthians 5:17 NRSV); "It is no longer I who live, but Christ lives in me" (Galatians 2:20 NKJV). The one I like most and use as an affirmation each day before I get out of bed is Colossians 1:27. I like to recite a slight paraphrase of the J. B. Phillips translation, inserting my name in the verse: "The secret is this, Nell Mohney: Christ alive in you bringing with him the hope of all the glorious things to come." When I encounter difficult situations or people, that verse is a reminder that I am not alone. I have resources far beyond myself. It was William Law, a wise and deeply spiritual man of the eighteenth century, who wrote: "A Christ not in you is a Christ not yours."

Receiving the Gift

Receiving this eternally significant gift is somewhat analogous to swimming. No one ever learns to swim by theory alone. The old story of the mother who said that her son wasn't going swimming until he learned to swim is nonsense. After the techniques of swimming have been explained and demonstrated, then we have to get in the water and trust ourselves to its supporting power. It cannot be proved without the personal experiment.

Receiving the gift of Christ in our lives means turning loose and surrendering ourselves, in the firm belief that whatever happens, he will hold us up. This is receiving not only the gift of salvation, but also the gift of victorious living. Joy is a by-product of this surrender. Why, then, are some people believers, but not very joyful ones? I am convinced this is because they have not invited Christ into every part of their being. Perhaps they have invited Christ into their minds but not into their emotions or wills. We must invite Christ into the library of our minds, the living room of our everyday activities, the playroom of our social lives, the dining room of our appetites, and the attic of our memories. And we invite him not as President for a short-term administration, but as King forever.

Once when our family was in England, we noticed that the flag of Great Britain always flies over Buckingham

Palace when the queen is in residence. The fruit of the Spirit—love, joy, peace, patience, kindness, generosity, faithfulness, gentleness, and self-control (Galatians 5:22-23)—are the flags that indicate Christ is in residence. Another evidence of Christ within is a pleasant facial expression. Dr. E. Stanley Jones once said that you are not responsible for the face you are born with, but you are responsible for the face you die with. Likewise, Gilbert Stuart, renowned English portrait painter, is reported to have said that by the time an individual reaches forty, that person's character has been undeniably written on his or her face.

In his book *The Secret of Radiant Living,* Dr. W. E. Sangster tells of a church official who paused briefly on the fringe of a Salvation Army open-air meeting. He was a grim-looking man with all the lines of his face running at acute angles. One of the Salvation Army lassies embarrassed this church official when she asked if he was saved. Drawing himself up to his full height, he replied in patronizing tones: "Well, I should hope so." The young girl called out to the leader: "He says he's saved, but what a face for a child of God."

We receive the gift of joy when we commit our lives to Christ. The more we open each of the rooms of our lives to him, the more we experience his joy. According to John 15:11, this is Christ's desire for us: "These things have I spoken unto you, that my joy might remain in you, and that your joy might be full."

Listen for the Sound of Trumpets

There is an old legend about Lucifer, the fallen angel. Someone asked what he missed most now that he no longer was in heaven. Without a moment's hesitation, he replied, "The sound of trumpets in the morning."

This story makes me think about the countless people

who get up, go to work, come home, watch television, go to bed, and get up to repeat the same routine. Their lives are mundane; they never hear the sound of trumpets in the morning. But the glorious truth is that despite our circumstances, joy can bubble up inside us. Despite the darkness of the night, "Joy comes in the morning" (Psalm 30:5 NKJV). This does not mean that we will never experience sadness or have bad things happen to us. Of course we will. This is part of the fabric of life. Yet even in the midst of difficulties, something inside us will sing, if only we listen for the sound of the trumpets.

How do we listen for the sound of the trumpets? How do we open ourselves to joyful opportunities and cultivate joy in our lives? In my own life, I have found three helpful ways to cultivate joy.

As I've mentioned throughout this book, reading affirmations from Scripture is an important way to be reminded of God's promises and filled with gratitude and joy. In addition to the Bible, I enjoy reading inspirational and motivational books and articles. Among the authors who help me experience joy are Catherine Marshall, E. Stanley Jones, Norman Vincent Peale, Robert Schuller, Maxie Dunnan, Bishop Earl Hunt, Charles Swindoll, and Max Lucado. You will have your own favorites. The important thing is to choose material that inspires and encourages you in the Spirit of Christ.

I also cultivate joy by associating with joyful people. If I am experiencing a down day, I try to telephone or see one of three friends whose joyful lives always seem to lift my spirits. Joy is a gift from God, and I have found that often it is delivered by a friend.

Another way I have found to cultivate joy is to keep a joy box. Have you ever received a card or letter that made you feel good or brought joy to your spirit? Put it in your very own joy box. Have you ever come across a cartoon that not only made you laugh but also gave you a larger perspective on your situation or problem? Cut it out and put it in your joy box. Have you ever come across a quotation in a book or the Bible that gave you a joyful spirit? Write it down and put it in your joy box. Then, on a "down day," open your box and let your spirit bubble with joy.

Stay Close to the Master of Joy

Jesus is the Master of Joy. When the angels announced Jesus' birth, they said, "Behold, I bring you good tidings of great joy" (Luke 2:10). Jesus continually sounded a note of joy in his life and teachings. He said that the kingdom of heaven is like a treasure someone finds "and for joy over it he goes and sells all that he has" (Matthew 13:44 NKJV). He also said to the disciples: "These things have I spoken unto you, that my joy might remain in you, and that your joy might be full" (John 15:11). Stay close to this Master of Joy. He will irradiate your personality with "joy unspeakable and full of glory" (1 Peter 1:8). As the late Dr. Samuel Shoemaker, a well-loved and distinguished clergyman, once wrote: "The surest mark of a Christian is not faith, or even love, but joy."

Steps for Acting with Joy

1. Begin each new day by affirming that joy is a choice. Remember this wisdom from Barbara Johnson: "Pain is inevitable, but misery is optional."

2. Remember that joy is not a human achievement. Lasting joy is not derived from good health, good circumstances, material possessions, or temperament.

3. Accept God's gift of joy. The gift of joy is Christ living within you, but you have to accept the gift. Remember William Law's words: "A Christ not in you is a Christ not yours."

4. Allow Christ to live in every part of your life: the library of your mind, the living room of your everyday activities, the playroom of your social life, the dining room of your appetites, and the attic of your memories. Christ wants to dwell in you—not as President but as King forever.

5. Find ways to listen for the "sound of trumpets in the morning," acknowledging that joy can bubble up inside you even in the midst of difficulties. Try reading inspirational material, associating with joyful people, and keeping a joy box.

6. When you are feeling down, repeat some of the following affirmations about joy: "The surest mark of a Christian is not faith, or even love, but joy" (Samuel Shoemaker); "The joy of the LORD is [my] strength" (Nehemiah 8:10); "These things have I spoken unto you, that my joy might remain in you, and that your joy might be full" (John 15:11).

7. Stay close to Christ, the Master of Joy. He will irradiate your personality with "joy unspeakable and full of glory" (1 Peter 1:8).

13.

ACT WITH FREEDOM

In the small North Carolina town in which I grew up, we celebrated the Fourth of July with gusto. There were parades with bands playing John Philip Sousa marches; there was a speech from one of our statesmen; and there was always a spectacular display of fireworks. It was common for townspeople to talk about national issues and even seek political office. When I was in high school, the governor of the state, a United States senator, and an ambassador to the Court of Saint James were all from our little town. It is not surprising, then, that celebrating our country's birthday was a big event in our town. Even today I never watch fireworks or sing the national anthem or other patriotic songs without being flooded with memories.

On the two-hundredth birthday of the United States, those memories were especially poignant. At our house we were also celebrating the birthday of our second son, Ralph, who was born on the third day of July. That day, July 4, 1976, he and his wife, Jackie, and their two young children, Ellen and Wesley, had dinner at our home. We watched television as the president spoke at Valley Forge and a fleet of tall ships sailed into New York harbor past the Statue of Liberty. The National Bicentennial Committee had asked every American to pray for our country before watching the brilliant display of fireworks at the Statue of Liberty. I remember giving thanks for two things: for our son, Ralph, whose life had brought us such joy; and for our country, praying we will always remember that its very foundation was laid in a belief in Almighty God. How vividly I remember thinking, "It doesn't get any better than this!" All the deep values of my life—love of God, love of family, and love of country—were included in our celebration that year.

Freedom Is a Universal Desire

There is something innate about the desire for freedom. No one would choose to be a slave, to be degraded, to be used as a doormat or treated as a second-class citizen. No one would choose to be a prisoner, to exchange the blue sky for a gray cell, where you are forced to spend hour upon miserable hour. Freedom is a universal desire.

Some years ago I heard a taped speech given by a Vietnam veteran, a returned prisoner of war. He told the story of having his plane shot down by the Viet Cong and landing in enemy territory. Because they were in a jungle, there was no prison; so they put him in a portable prison, which they dragged with them from place to place. It was a tiger's cage made of bamboo. It measured five feet by four feet; he was six feet two inches tall. He lived there for three years. Only on rare occasions did the guards allow him to slide through the door of the cage to stretch his legs.

For months he was so depressed that he lay in a heap on the floor of that cage. In despair he began to pray, and hope began to rise within his heart. He dreamed of the day he would be free again. One day he began to think of escape. When the guards were sleeping, he tried to loosen one of the bamboo poles on the side of the cage. It was painstakingly slow work, for he was constantly surrounded by guards.

The night came when he was able to remove the pole. His heart raced; the fear of being caught produced a lump in his throat and a knot in his stomach. But his work wasn't finished. Though he was only a shadow of the two-hundred-forty-five-pound man he once had been, he couldn't pull himself through the opening. Slowly he began to work on another pole, and then another.

Finally the night came when he was able to pull his emaciated body between the bamboo poles and escape into freedom. Weak from fear and physical deterioration, he managed to pull himself into an upright position and stagger farther into the jungle. To his advantage, it was a black, starless night. After several days without food, he was picked up by American airmen and flown to safety.

It was a gripping story, told so graphically that I found myself sitting on the edge of my chair. His closing comment seared itself into my mind and continues to resurface in unexpected moments all these years later: "All of you look well fed and well clothed, but I wonder how many of you are living in prisons of your own making?" Even though we all desire freedom, many of us still lock ourselves in prisons of our own making—prisons of hatred, jealousy, selfishness, resentment, addiction, deceit, guilt, purposelessness, depression, and sin. But it doesn't have to be that way. Christ offers us a way out.

Freedom Is an Inside Job

No matter how hard we work, we can never break out of prison on our own. We can straighten the cell and rearrange the meager furnishings, but only Christ holds the key. "If the Son makes you free, you shall be free indeed" (John 8:36 NKJV).

Even so, freedom is definitely an inside job. We have to *choose* to accept the key to freedom offered us by Jesus Christ: "You shall know the truth, and the truth shall make you free" (John 8:32 NKJV). The truth of which Jesus speaks is that we cannot set ourselves free. Only Jesus can free us from the things we so easily become enslaved by—things such as habits, relationships, dependencies, and circumstances.

The Magna Carta of Spiritual Freedom

In a world that continually drags us down and enslaves us, there is no way we can be "up" until we issue our "declaration of dependence" upon Christ and stay in close fellowship with him. Then and only then are we free from slavery and imprisoned living.

During one of his missionary journeys, Paul ministered to the people of Galatia, who were enslaved by their fears, superstitions, passions, and instincts. Then they accepted the liberating power of Christ, and they found the joyful liberty that comes with the certainty of God's love and forgiveness. But after Paul left, other Christians came and confused the issue. They insisted that the new Christians at Galatia must be circumcised and must keep the Sabbath and the new moon and other practices of the Jews.

Confused by the new information, the Galatians were tempted to be ruled by legalism and negative restrictions. Paul learned of this and reacted with sternness, writing the letter to the Galatians found in our Scriptures. He reminded them that they had been delivered from legalism and no longer were bound by it. Included in the letter is the verse that has come to be claimed by individuals and nations alike as the Magna Carta of spiritual freedom for all humanity: "Christ has set us free. Stand firm, therefore, and do not submit again to a yoke of slavery" (Galatians 5:1 NRSV).

You Don't Have to Earn Your Freedom

Christ sets us free—free from sin, guilt, fear, and negative living. The truth of this gift of grace didn't become apparent to me for many years. I grew up in a church where there were lots of don'ts. Don't do this or you will be punished; don't do that or you will go to hell. One of my most vivid memories is of being seven years old and afraid to pray: "Now I lay me down to sleep, I pray the Lord my soul to keep. If I should die before I wake, I pray the Lord my soul to take."

My second grade Sunday school teacher, in what I now realize was an attempt to keep seven-year-olds seated and quiet, drew a graphic picture of a frightening God. She told us that God was a great big man who wore a big black robe and sat behind a big black desk. He had a big black book with everybody's name in it. Every time we did anything wrong, he put a big black mark by our names. When we got enough black marks, he marked us off the book. For imaginative second graders, that meant death, and we became terrified of dying.

When my mother finally persuaded me to tell her why I no longer wanted to pray, she marched down to the minister's office and told him what had happened. Just that week he had heard the same story from other parents, and the teacher was "promoted" to the adult division. After that experience, it took me years to perceive of God as loving and forgiving, as portrayed by Jesus. Incidentally, another outcome of that experience was my deep fear of our minister, a large man who wore a black robe when he preached!

Fortunately for me, our next pastor was a short man of slight build who wore a gray robe. He also had a wonderful twinkle in his eye and a contagious laugh. He loved people, and we soon adored him. For me, he broke the fearful image of a stern, unforgiving God. Though it took me a long time to understand and live in the grace of

God, rather than try to measure up to the harsh, rigid, unremitting demands of an angry God, eventually I came to know that God's love and mercy are all-encompassing. We don't earn God's forgiving love; we simply accept it. Of course, God has high standards of excellence for those who seek to live in the kingdom of God; by God's very nature, his standards have to be high and noble. But God loves us with an everlasting love, and believing this sets us free.

Actualizing Your Freedom

I've become aware of how often I hear the following phrases on television, in the movies, and in real life: "I feel empty"; "I'm burned out"; "Life is meaningless (or boring, or unbearable)." I am reminded that one of our greatest freedoms is the freedom to become what we were meant to be—to actualize our God-given capacities.

Saint Augustine said that asking yourself this question is the first step toward maturity: "What do I want to be remembered for?" This is far more than just a wispy, wishful question. It cuts to the very essence of our personalities and souls. This is what Stephen Covey means in his book *Seven Habits of Highly Effective People* when he says that we should begin with the end in mind.

As I shared in chapter 4, Peter Drucker, business consultant and author, suggests that we set ultimate goals for our lives, and then see that our short- and long-term goals work toward this end. When I heard him say that some twenty years ago, I spent hours in soul-searching, personality evaluation, and study of God's Word. I also spent a lot of time writing, condensing, and sharpening my ultimate goals. It's a powerful exercise, one I recommend for your own personal fulfillment. (Steps for this exercise are found on page 59.) I finally came up with four ultimate goals, each with its own short- and long-term goals:

My Ultimate Goals

1. To be an authentic Christian.

2. To give and receive love—especially to the significant others in my life.

3. To use my talents of writing and speaking to help, encourage, and serve others in the name of Christ.

4. To go to heaven when I die.

These goals have become the mission statement that provides direction and purpose for my daily living.

In his book *Half Time—Changing Your Game Plan from Success to Significance,* Bob Buford gives the same idea a slightly different twist. He suggests that we decide what we want for our epitaph. He says that on his own tombstone, he would like to have the following: "Robert Buford—100 x." This comes from Jesus' parable of the sower recorded in Matthew 13:3-9. A farmer went forth to sow seeds. Some fell on the path, and birds ate them. Some fell on rocky places where the soil was shallow. The seeds began to sprout, but they couldn't develop roots because of the shallow soil. Some fell among thorns, which grew up and choked the plants. Others fell on good soil and produced a crop—some one hundred, some sixty, and some thirty times. Bob Buford wants his life to be good soil in which the seeds of God's purposes are planted and the harvest is one hundred times what was sown.

Freedom is sometimes hard to actualize, and the parable of the sower tells us why. To me, the birds eating the seed represents the distractions that don't allow God's purposes to grow in our lives. Our desires to have and to achieve distract us from the deep-seated need to be all that God intended us to be. Society's pressure, particularly through the media and advertising, keeps us glued to having and doing. Often it's not until we reach midlife that the sense of emptiness emerges. Rather than face ourselves as spiritual beings, too many of us try to escape through alcohol, drugs, affairs, or conformity.

The shallow soil represents the fact that often we haven't cultivated the spiritual soil. We are believers, but our lives are so overstuffed with activities that there is no room or time for cultivating the gospel message. We don't turn away from Christ, but like the innkeeper in Bethlehem, our hearts say, "There is no room—for his message, for his spirit, for his freedom."

The thorns represent life's difficulties. What do you do when life says "no"? The "no" can come in the form of a rebellious child, a chronic illness, a job loss, a divorce, the death of a loved one, or a sense of meaninglessness. Some people are so rooted in the central certainties that they bounce back with an even greater vitality. Some, however, bog down in bitterness and anger and grief. They withdraw from life or put their lives on hold. The thorns have choked the spiritual life out of them. The people who ultimately receive Christ's freedom and produce a great harvest are those who keep the soil cultivated and allow Christ to work within them.

The opportunity to actualize our God-given capacities is a wonderful freedom. It involves asking the question, "For what do I want to be remembered?" It involves determining our ultimate goals. And it involves being forever on guard to ensure that God's seeds of freedom fall on good soil.

Retaining Your Freedom

In order to retain the freedom offered us by Christ, we must remain honest with ourselves, with God, and with others. The Bible tells us the story of David, who in his youth and young adulthood stayed in close relationship with God. In midlife, however, he fell into self-deception and sinned. Later, bitterly regretting what he had done, he wrote: "Behold, thou desirest truth in the inward parts" (Psalm 51:6). All of us seem to have a limitless capacity for self-deception. It is difficult to see ourselves as we really are.

The Scottish poet Robert Burns was sitting in church one day when he saw something unusual about the woman sitting in the pew ahead of him. She was beautiful and elegantly dressed—and she knew it! She was wearing a brand-new, balloon-shaped bonnet, across which a fat, gray louse, plump as a gooseberry, was slowly crawling.

He later wrote his now famous poem "To a Louse—On Seeing One on a Lady's Bonnet in Church," which ends with this prayer:

> O wad some Power the giftie gie us
> To see oursels as ithers see us!
> It wad frae mony a blunder free us.

It's true that when we see ourselves as others see us, we are freed from our own self-deception. Honesty begins within. Unless we are honest with ourselves, we cannot be honest with others. As William Shakespeare wrote in *Hamlet*, "This above all, to thine own self be true. And it must follow as the night the day, thou canst not then be false to any man."

Be Honest with Yourself

Once at a seminar I spent a long time talking with a recovering alcoholic. She reminded me that the first step in Alcoholics Anonymous is total honesty. She said: "We have to admit that we are powerless over alcohol." Then I remembered that the organization itself began with an experience of total honesty.

In 1935, two men met in Akron, Ohio. One was "Dr. Bob," who became addicted to alcohol during his twenties and went to psychiatrist Carl Jung for help. Dr. Jung told him that his problem was beyond the reach of psychiatry, that the only thing that could save him was a religious conversion. Dr. Bob followed this "prescription." He experienced the miracle of a spiritual rebirth, thereby discovering that the power of God could do what nothing else could. With God's help, he was able to stop drinking.

The other man, a drinking buddy of Dr. Bob, was named Bill Wilson. Bill also was an alcoholic, which had caused him to develop cirrhosis of the liver. When Bill went to his doctor for help, he was told that medicine could not help him. All his life he had put his faith in science. Now he felt that he had been worshiping a god that turned out to be as helpless as a wooden idol. The doctor said the only thing that could help Bill was to stop drinking, and that was the one thing he could not do.

Upon meeting Dr. Bob in Akron, Bill invited him to a bar, as usual, and was surprised to learn that his friend had stopped drinking. When he asked his friend how he had done it, Dr. Bob replied, "Through the power of God." This was no consolation to Bill, because he did not believe in God. Still, he had an open mind.

When Bill was later hospitalized, with no prospect but death before him, he said a desperate and unusual prayer. It went something like this: "O God, if there is a God, help me!" That night, after that honest prayer, Bill felt a wind from beyond space blowing through him and a light beyond the stars shining into his soul. Somehow he knew that God was there and would help him. In fact, God did help him withdraw completely from his dependence on alcohol.

The two men got together soon afterward, and through a process of trial and error and prayer, they worked out the Twelve Steps and the basic organization of Alcoholics

Anonymous. As a result, millions of people have been helped to sobriety and led to God.

Just as being honest with themselves—admitting that they were addicted to alcohol and that they needed help—was the first step for these men, so also we must be honest with ourselves. We must see ourselves as we are, admit our sin, and reach out to God.

Be Honest with God

Not only do we seem to have a relentless capacity for self-deceit, but we also seem to have an uncanny ability to "shave the truth" with God. Remember Adam and Eve? When they disobeyed and ate the forbidden fruit, they didn't confess their sin to God. They tried to hide from God. When God confronted them face-to-face, they played the "blame game."

Adam said that he had eaten the fruit, but that it wasn't his fault: "The woman whom thou gavest to be with me, she gave me of the tree" (Genesis 3:12). In turn, Eve said, "The serpent beguiled me, and I did eat" (v. 13). A speaker I once heard said: "And the serpent didn't have a leg to stand on!"

Like Adam and Eve, we too tend to blame others for our mistakes, our faults, and our failures. In a seminar I conducted on "Being All God Meant Us to Be," I heard excuses such as: "I could live up to my potential if I weren't married to such a louse"; "My drinking has resulted from having four teenagers. They are driving me nuts"; "I came from a dysfunctional family, and I simply can't control my temper." It is so much easier to blame others than to take responsibility for our own actions. But God knows us through and through. He loves us and, if we sincerely ask, will cleanse our thoughts and empower us for living. One of my favorite prayers is an ancient one, but it is as relevant as the morning newspaper for my life:

Almighty God, unto Whom all hearts are open, all desires
known and from Whom no secrets are hid,
Cleanse the thoughts of our hearts by the inspiration of
Thy Holy Spirit,
That we may perfectly love Thee and worthily magnify
Thy Holy Name.

A number of years ago, a friend told me of having attended a three-day seminar on healing presented by Ruth Carter Stapleton. At the beginning of the seminar, Mrs. Stapleton told this story. It seems that just before the first session, as Mrs. Stapleton was sitting at the back of the auditorium, a short, elderly man sat down beside her and told her why he had come. He said that he was not a Christian, but that he had awakened from sleep two nights before when a voice out of nowhere said distinctly: "Jesus Christ." After seeing the announcements of the meeting, he had to come. Just as the stranger told her this, Mrs. Stapleton had to go forward to speak. That evening and for the next three days she spoke about Jesus and his unconditional love, and at every meeting the stranger was present.

At the end of the seminar, when Ruth invited people to meet with her, the man was among those who came forward. He told her an amazing story. More than thirty years before, he said, he had gone by boat to another country to work at what he thought would be a good job in a resort hotel. On his arrival, he found that his only pay for scrubbing the floors, lighting the furnace each morning, and doing other chores would be room and board. Disillusioned and disgusted with the situation, he decided he would take the next boat home.

The following morning he tried to light the furnace as he had been instructed, but only some of the burners ignited. Since they seemed to be burning well, he turned them up, went to his room, took his suitcase with all his belongings, and left the hotel for the long voyage home.

He was half a block away when he heard an explosion. As he looked back he saw that the hotel was an inferno, flames and smoke belching from its broken windows. Then he ran to his boat. He never found out how many lives had been ended in the explosion.

"I've been running ever since," the man told Mrs. Stapleton. For thirty years, he said, he had lived in hell as he thought of the destruction he must have inadvertently wrought. "Do you think," he asked her, "that Christ can forgive me for what I did?" Mrs. Stapleton assured the man that Jesus had died for all the sins of the world and that he would indeed forgive him this awesome misdeed if the man confessed it to him. He began to sob as the truth sank in. Then he said, "It's gone." He explained that ever since that day of the explosion he had been plagued with a lump in his throat, and now it was gone; and for the first time in three decades, also gone were his guilt and shame. His honest confession brought about healing without and within.

How often we live only half lives, imprisoned by real or imagined guilt. Or, like the man who sought help from Mrs. Stapleton, we spend our lives trying to run away from guilt. Evidence of this may be seen in feverish activities, compulsive buying, use of alcohol and drugs, illicit sex, and depression. The way out, of course, is always to be honest with God, confess our guilt, and receive his forgiveness.

Be Honest with Others

One of the great values in meeting in small groups for Christian fellowship and study is the opportunity to articulate our fears, our hopes, our pain, and our joys to other Christians whom we trust. It is an adventure in accountability and burden-bearing. In his book *The Miracle of Dialogue*, Ruel Howe says that in talking through our problems and differences, we are able to see situations more clearly and heal the hurts that they have caused.

Marian and I have been friends for years. She has many good qualities, including a generous spirit. If there is a death in her neighborhood, Marian will stay up half the night preparing food for the family. She is willing to do whatever it takes to help in a time of need.

One of her less appealing characteristics, which seems to increase with age, is an irritating habit of talking too much about herself and bragging about her family and possessions. I believe this stems from a deep-seated sense of inferiority which causes her to overcompensate. Whatever the cause, the habit is destructive and causes others to see her as arrogant and self-centered.

As her friend, I knew I needed to talk honestly with Marian about this, but I also knew how sensitive she is. Because I value our friendship and didn't want to disrupt it, I prayed earnestly about the best approach. It was provided!

One day she surprised me by asking, "Do you think I am 'snooty'?"

Caught off guard, I said, "Why do you ask?" Then she told me that someone had said that to her. She was hurt and surprised. In fact, she had been totally blind to this aspect of her personality.

I replied, "Down deep you are a warm, generous, wonderful person, but sometimes you give the impression of being arrogant." This opened the door for an honest "carefrontation." Always eager to grow and learn, Marian took the conversation seriously and began to make a one-hundred-eighty-degree turn.

The "miracle of dialogue" can help each of us to see ourselves more clearly. When we are honest with others and hold one another accountable in the spirit of Christ, we help one another to be honest with ourselves and with God. Only then can we actualize and retain our greatest freedom—the freedom to become all God created us to be.

Steps for Acting with Freedom

1. Remember that real freedom comes when Christ is Lord in our lives. "If the Son makes you free, you shall be free indeed" (John 8:36 NKJV).

2. Realize that it is easy to revert to self-imposed prisons. When you are tempted, affirm the Magna Carta of spiritual freedom: "Christ has set us free. Stand firm, therefore, and do not submit again to a yoke of slavery" (Galatians 5:1 NRSV).

3. Ask yourself if you are living in a prison of your own making. *Choose* to accept the key to freedom offered you by Jesus Christ.

4. With the help of God and suggestions in this book, determine a plan of action. This may involve forgiveness, restitution, self-discipline, participating in a support group, or something else. It definitely will involve staying in close daily fellowship with Christ.

5 Remember Christ sets you free *for* something: being all that you were created to be.

6. Ask yourself Saint Augustine's question: "What do I want to be remembered for?"

7. Begin work on your ultimate goals. Then put the goals into daily practice.

8. Remember that there are three things required of you if you are to claim spiritual freedom: being honest with yourself, being honest with God, and being honest with others.

9. Reread the parable of the sower (Matthew 13:3-9). Determine the thorns that are choking out the Christian faith in your life. Begin now to destroy them.

A FINAL WORD

Throughout this book, I have given you a formula for being up on down days. It is far more than learning a magic strategy or gimmick. It is a lifestyle that is rooted in a solid, personal relationship with Jesus Christ. It requires a positive mind-set, a belief in yourself as a person of worth, a good sense of humor, and a determination to act with joy and freedom. There is only one other essential attribute: a commitment to keep on keeping on.

Many years ago Margaret Johnson wrote a book titled *When God Says "No."* Though the book is now out of print, the message of three stories from the book continues to encourage me when I feel like quitting. I pass these stories on to you in the hope that their message will bring you encouragement, too.

The first story is from Margaret Johnson's childhood. When she was in elementary school, her mother took her and several of her friends to the creek for a picnic. Since none of them could swim, she asked the girls not to go near the water. While playing, one of the children inadvertently stepped over the bank and fell into a deep section of the water. Thinking quickly, Margaret's mother climbed a tree, leaned out over the water from one of the lower limbs, and caught the girl's hand. Mrs. Johnson quietly reassured her by saying, "Hold on, honey." Soon help arrived. A man swam to the child and brought her safely into shore. A tragedy had been adverted by quick thinking and sound advice: "Hold on, honey."

The second story is about an episode that happened shortly after Margaret's mother had come home from the hospital with a new baby. The cradle was placed in the den near the open fireplace. Once while checking on the baby, Mrs. Johnson stepped too close to the fire and her long flannel robe caught fire. Margaret heard her father scream, "Don't run, Maggie! Don't run!" Grabbing a quilt from the closet, Mr. Johnson took his wife in his arms and smothered the flames with a quilt. As he did this, he said, "Thank God you didn't run, Maggie."

The third story is about an experience that happened when Margaret's father was dying of cancer at home. He was a huge man, and they had hired male attendants to lift and care for him. One day around noon when the attendant had gone to lunch, Mr. Johnson decided he wanted to see his rose garden. Explaining that she and Margaret could not get him to the porch, Mrs. Johnson said that he would have to wait until the attendant returned. Mr. Johnson insisted that he wanted to go immediately. He convinced his wife that if he could place one arm around each of their shoulders for support, he could walk to the front porch.

Though they were skeptical, the women decided to give it a try. Mr. Johnson had taken only two steps when his knees began to give way. Realizing that they couldn't lift him back into bed, Mrs. Johnson said slowly and quietly, "Take one step more—just one step more." Step by painful step, the dying man followed his wife's instructions. They put him in a chair on the porch where he enjoyed the roses until the attendant helped him back to bed. He died two hours later—but he had seen the beauty of his roses.

When life is difficult and you are feeling down, put your faith in Christ, then hold on, don't run, and take one step more.

BIBLICAL AFFIRMATIONS

Courage / Confidence

In quietness and in confidence shall be [my] strength. (Isaiah 30:15)

They that wait upon the LORD shall renew their strength; they shall mount up with wings as eagles; they shall run, and not be weary; and they shall walk, and not faint. (Isaiah 40:31)

If God be for [me], who can be against [me]? (Romans 8:31)

In all these things we are more than conquerors through Him who loved us. (Romans 8:37 NKJV)

Christ has set us free. Stand firm, therefore, and do not submit again to a yoke of slavery. (Galatians 5:1)

He who has begun a good work in you will complete it. (Philippians 1:6 NKJV)

"I can do all things through Christ who strengthens me." (Philippians 4:13 NKJV)

Hope / Assurance of God's Love

For God so loved [substitute your name], that he gave his only Son, so that everyone who believes in him may not perish but may have eternal life. (John 3:16 NRSV)

Who shall separate us from the love of Christ? (Romans 8:35)

And now abide faith, hope, love, these three; but the greatest of these is love. (1 Corinthians 13:13 NKJV)

The God of love and peace shall be with you. (2 Corinthians 13:11)

The secret is simply this: . . . Christ [is] in [us] bringing with him the hope of all the glorious things to come. (Colossians 1:27 J. B. Phillips)

Hope is the anchor of the soul. (Hebrews 6:19, paraphrase)

I will never leave you nor forsake you. (Hebrews 13:5 NKJV)

Peace / Rest

Be still, and know that I am God. (Psalm 46:10)

Thou wilt keep him in perfect peace, whose mind is stayed on thee. (Isaiah 26:3)

"Come to me, all you who are weary and burdened, and I will give you rest." (Matthew 11:28 NIV)

"My peace I give unto you: not as the world giveth, give I unto you. Let not your heart be troubled, neither let it be afraid." (John 14:27)

Gratitude / Praise

This is the day which the LORD hath made; [I] will rejoice and be glad in it. (Psalm 118:24)

I will praise thee; for I am fearfully and wonderfully made. (Psalm 139:14)

In every thing give thanks. (1 Thessalonians 5:18)

Joy / Laughter

A merry heart doeth good like a medicine. (Proverbs 17:22)

"I have come that [you] may have life, and that [you] may have it more abundantly." (John 10:10)

"These things have I spoken unto you, that my joy might remain in you, and that your joy might be full." (John 15:11)

Now the God of hope fill you with all joy and peace in believing. (Romans 15:13)

Trust / Faith

Trust in the LORD with all thine heart; and lean not unto thine own understanding. In all thy ways acknowledge him, and he shall direct thy paths. (Proverbs 3:5-6)

With God all things are possible. (Matthew 19:26)

"Lo, I am with you always, even unto the end of the age." (Matthew 28:20)